SESE Programme

Small World

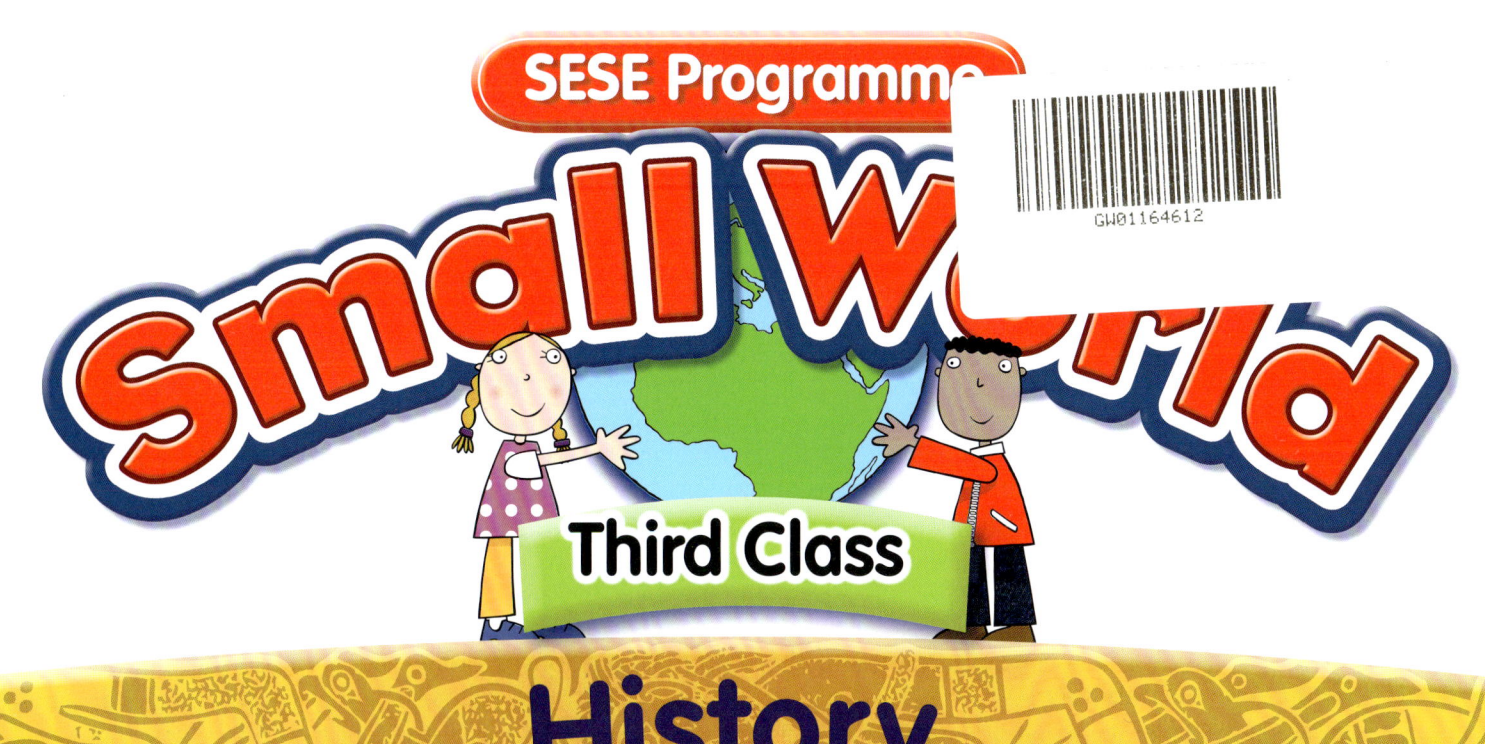

Third Class

History

CJ Fallon
ESTABLISHED 1895

Introduction

Small World History is a series of history textbooks, activity books, teacher's manuals and corresponding **digital resources**. It adheres to the Revised Primary Curriculum and has been written, researched and class tested by primary teachers. The corresponding **Curriculum Strands** and **Strand Units** are listed throughout.

The *Small World* History textbook accompanies the combined *Small World* **Geography & Science textbook**. Both books are linked to create the integrated and thematic approach that constitutes SESE.

Small World History has been designed to cover the relevant curricular areas over the course of the **two-year period** suggested in the Curriculum. It also allows for these topics to be covered **chronologically**.

The increased emphasis on **literacy** is catered for in the series with units following a four- or six-page format, providing ample opportunities for reading. New **vocabulary** is introduced at the start of each unit and there is a **glossary** of historical terms at the end of each book.

The use of **timelines** at the start of each unit follow the scaffolding approach of starting with what the pupils already know. Events worldwide are compared to events in Ireland during the same time period.

Each unit in the textbook has a page of activities at the end and selected units feature **intermittent questions**. These activities encompass: writing summaries, debating a motion, timeline activities, drawing maps and diagrams, brainstorming, higher order questions, creative ideas, **cause and effect**, and historical vocabulary.

The **teacher's digital version** of the textbook has hot-spot links to videos, images and audio. These links are **embedded in the text**, giving a multimedia approach that brings History to life.

The **activity book** that accompanies the series requires children to 'work as a historian'. They are given opportunities to compare evidence by examining documents and photographs. There is also a range of sequencing and timeline activities, plus ideas for creating **empathy** with characters. The **local studies** templates and family trees will ensure that the child's personal responses are recorded and the **self-assessment** feature enables the child to monitor his/her own progress.

Author: Déirdre Kirwan, Maureen O'Hara
Editor: Donna Garvin
Design and layout: Annick Doza
Illustrations: Kerry Ingham (GCI); Tim Hutchinson
Photographs: Alamy; Glow Images; Thinkstock; Wikimedia; Newgrange © National Monuments Service (Department of Arts, Heritage and the Gaeltacht)

Published by
CJ Fallon
Ground Floor, Block B
Liffey Valley Office Campus
Dublin 22

ISBN 978-0-7144-1904-6

First edition March 2013
This reprint April 2021

© CJ Fallon

All rights reserved

No part of this publication may be reproduced or transmitted, in any form or by any means, electronic, mechanical, photocopying or otherwise, without the prior written permission of the publisher.

Printed in Ireland by
W&G Baird Ltd
Caulside Drive
Antrim BT41 2RS

Contents

Unit	Title	Strand	Strand Unit	Page
1	Fionn and the Fianna	Story	Myths and Legends	4
2	The Stone Age	Early People and Ancient Societies	Stone Age Peoples	10
3	Food and Farming	Continuity and Change Over Time	Food and Farming	16
4	People of the Tigris and Euphrates Rivers	Early People and Ancient Societies	Early Societies of the Tigris and Euphrates Valleys	22
5	Setanta	Story	Myths and Legends	28
6	Games and Pastimes	Local Studies	Games and Pastimes in the Past	32
7	The Bronze Age	Early People and Ancient Societies	Bronze Age Peoples	36
8	Saint Brendan	Story	Myths and Legends	42
9	The Egyptians	Early People and Ancient Societies	Egyptians	46
10	The Wooden Horse of Troy	Story	Myths and Legends	50
11	Schools and Education	Continuity and Change Over Time	Schools and Education	54
12	King Arthur and Excalibur	Story	Myths and Legends	60
13	Life in Norman Ireland	Life, Society, Work and Culture in the Past	Life in Norman Ireland	64
14	Life in Medieval Towns	Life, Society, Work and Culture in the Past	Life in Medieval Towns and Countryside in Ireland and Europe	70
15	Christopher Columbus	Story	Stories from the Lives of People in the Past	76
16	Transport	Continuity and Change Over Time	Transport	80
17	Tom Crean	Story	Stories from the Lives of People in the Past	86
18	My Family	Local Studies	My Family	92
	Glossary			96

Unit 1: Fionn and the Fianna

New Words
knowledge   wisdom   motto   blister   Samhain   banquet   goblin   hazel

1 Long ago, a wise, old poet called Finnéigeas lived in a hut on the bank of the River Boyne. He lived there all alone and he spent his time reading books and writing poetry.

2 A famous salmon lived in the River Boyne. It was a huge fish with golden scales and it was known as the Salmon of Knowledge. People said that whoever was first to eat the flesh of the salmon would be given the gift of wisdom. Finnéigeas longed to catch the salmon so that he would get the gift of wisdom.

3 One day, as Finnéigeas was fishing, a fair-haired boy came walking towards him.

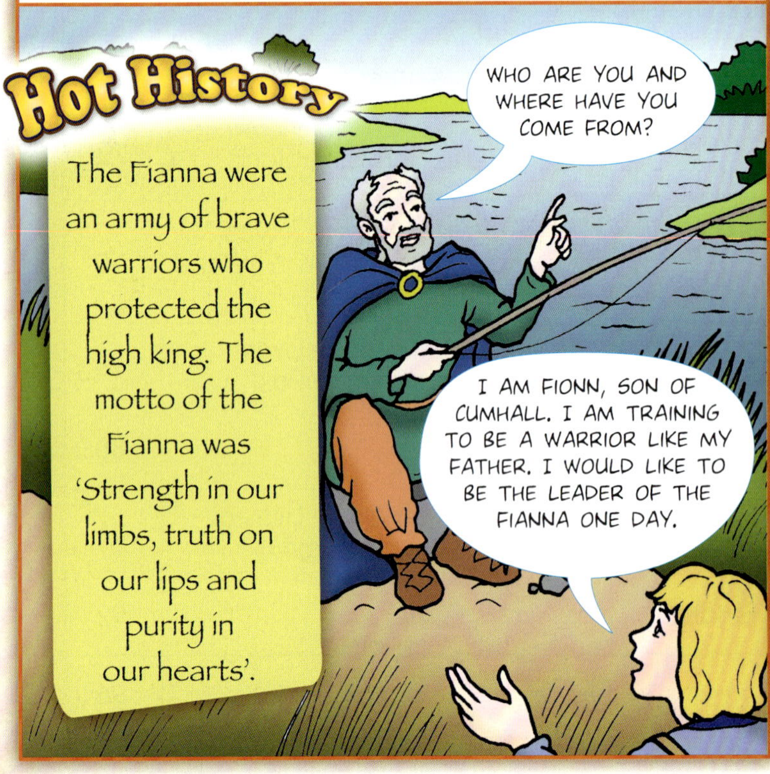

WHO ARE YOU AND WHERE HAVE YOU COME FROM?

I AM FIONN, SON OF CUMHALL. I AM TRAINING TO BE A WARRIOR LIKE MY FATHER. I WOULD LIKE TO BE THE LEADER OF THE FIANNA ONE DAY.

Hot History
The Fianna were an army of brave warriors who protected the high king. The motto of the Fianna was 'Strength in our limbs, truth on our lips and purity in our hearts'.

4 In those days, there were no schools in Ireland. Instead of going to school, young warriors were taught by wise men like Finnéigeas. They were taught poetry, storytelling and many other skills.

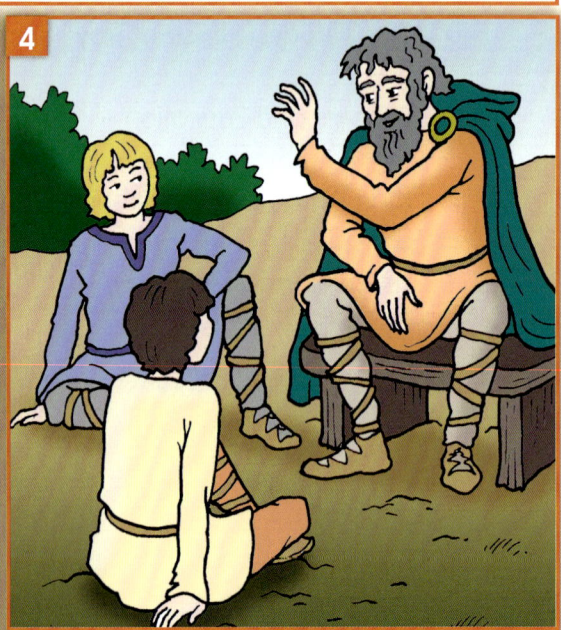

Strand: Story   Strand Unit: Myths and Legends

5. Fionn lived happily with the old man. At night he listened to Finnéigeas's stories about famous heroes and battles. During the day, Fionn cooked the meals and kept the hut warm and clean.

6. One day, Finnéigeas saw the huge, powerful salmon swimming in the river. He was very excited and he ran to get a strong net to catch it. Finnéigeas knew that if anyone looked in the salmon's eyes, that person would fall into a deep sleep.

7. For hours, he tried to catch the powerful fish, but it was too strong and too fast for him. Suddenly the salmon jumped high up into the air and looked into Finnéigeas's eyes!

8. Finnéigeas could not help staring at the fish and he fell asleep at once. Fionn ran out from the hut and he saw what had happened. He woke Finnéigeas before the salmon escaped. Finnéigeas covered his eyes with a cloth and he put the net in the river again.

9. For hours and hours, he tried to catch the fish, but each time he failed. As night was falling, he decided to have one last try. Finally, he got lucky and he managed to catch the great fish.

10. "I HAVE WAITED SO LONG TO CATCH THE SALMON OF KNOWLEDGE AND NOW AT LAST I HAVE DONE IT!"

Fionn and Finnéigeas prepared the salmon and then they put it on a spit over the fire.

Strand: Story Strand Unit: Myths and Legends

11

I AM GOING TO COLLECT WILD BERRIES TO EAT WITH THE FISH. I WILL RETURN VERY SOON. MAKE SURE YOU DO NOT EAT ANY OF THE FISH.

Finnéigeas told Fionn to watch the salmon closely and to be careful that it did not burn.

12

Hot History

Fionn also received the gift of healing from the salmon. He could heal a sick or wounded person by giving them a drink of water from his cupped hands.

As the fish cooked, a big blister appeared on its back. Fionn pressed the blister and it burst, but in doing so, he burned his thumb. He put his thumb in his mouth to stop the pain and without realising it, he was the first person to taste the Salmon of Knowledge.

13 When Finnéigeas returned, he saw a strange look on Fionn's face. When Fionn told him what had happened, the old man's face dropped. At first Finnéigeas was very disappointed, because he knew that now he would never be the wisest man in Ireland.

YOU ARE NOW VERY WISE, BECAUSE YOU HAVE RECEIVED THE GIFT OF WISDOM FROM THE SALMON OF KNOWLEDGE.

14 However, he was happy after all, that it was Fionn, his favourite student, who had got the gift of knowledge.

GO TO TARA AND JOIN THE FIANNA AND YOU WILL BECOME THE GREATEST LEADER THE FIANNA HAS EVER KNOWN.

Fionn said goodbye to his old friend and teacher and he headed off for Tara.

Strand: Story   Strand Unit: Myths and Legends

15 Samhain was an important festival in ancient Ireland. It was held on November 1st to mark the end of the grazing season. Fionn arrived at Tara in time for the feast of Samhain. The High King of Ireland and the Fianna were gathered for a banquet. As night began to fall, everyone became quiet. The king rose and they all knew that he was going to talk about the Goblin of Tara.

16 The Goblin of Tara was a fiery monster that appeared in Tara during the feast of Samhain. As the monster came near Tara, he would play magical music that made everyone fall asleep. Then he would breath fire from his mouth and burn everything to the ground. Nobody knew how to stop the monster.

Can anybody save us?

17 They all agreed that only the best warrior could stop the fierce monster and lead the Fianna. Fionn had a magic spear that was made by the fairies. He knew it would protect him from the music.

I will stop the monster but if I do, you must make me leader of the Fianna.

18 As soon as he heard the goblin's harp, Fionn began to feel drowsy. He pressed the magic spear against his forehead and he no longer heard the music. His strength returned and he was wide awake. The goblin reached the palace, blowing flames from its mouth.

19 Fionn kept beating out the fire with his cloak before it reached the wooden walls. The goblin turned and fled and Fionn hurled his magic spear at him. The goblin fell dead on the ground.

Fionn had saved Tara and he became the leader of the Fianna from that day.

Strand: Story **Strand Unit:** Myths and Legends

Tests for Joining the Fianna

To join the Fianna, a warrior had to pass the following tests:

1. Jump over a branch as tall as yourself. 
2. Run under a stick placed at the height of your knees. 
3. Pick a thorn from your foot as you run at top speed. 
4. Run through the forest without breaking even one stick under your feet, or tearing your clothes on a bush. 
5. Know 12 books of poetry off by heart. 
6. Promise to obey the **Rules of the Fianna**. 
7. Stand in a hole up to your waist and defend yourself against nine warriors, using only a shield and a hazel stick.

Strand: Story Strand Unit: Myths and Legends

ACTIVITIES

A. Can You Remember?

1. What was the name of Fionn's father?
2. What kind of things did the wise men teach their pupils?
3. Who were the Fianna?
4. How could Fionn cure a sick person?
5. Why was it a bad idea to look into the salmon's eyes?
6. How was the salmon cooked?

B. Choose the Correct Answer to Complete Each Sentence.

1. The Salmon of Knowledge had the gift of _____.
   A. health and wealth, B. wisdom and knowledge, or C. power and knowledge
2. Finnéigeas told stories about _____.
   A. heroes and battles, B. warriors and witches, or C. ghosts and goblins
3. When Finnéigeas looked into the salmon's eyes, _____.
   A. he fell asleep, B. he caught it, or C. he cooked it
4. Finnéigeas spent many hours _____.
   A. trying to catch the salmon, B. swimming in the river, or C. talking about the Fianna
5. To finally catch the salmon, Finnéigeas had to _____.
   A. put a cloth over his eyes, B. use a better fishing rod, or C. find a rowing boat

C. Think About It.

1. Do you think it was a good idea for Fionn to watch the salmon as it cooked?
2. Do you think the Fianna had a good life?
3. What do you think the **Rules of the Fianna** were? Write three rules.
4. Do you think it was fair that Fionn got the gift of knowledge?

D. Get Creative.

1. Tell the story of how you became a member of the Fianna. Describe how you passed the tests.
2. Act out the conversation that took place between Finnéigeas and Fionn, when Fionn told him that he had put his thumb in his mouth.
3. Why do you think Fionn got a magic spear from the fairies? Tell the story.

E. Digging Deeper

1. Read the book, *Celtic Tales of Enchantment* by Liam Mac Uistin (O'Brien Press).
2. Use the internet to watch a video of the legend of the Salmon of Knowledge. Your teacher will give you a list of words to key into a search engine.

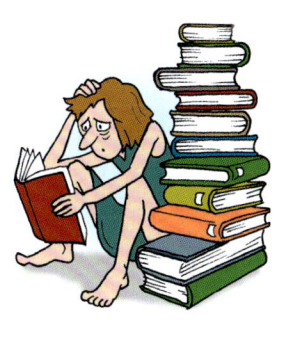

Strand: Story   Strand Unit: Myths and Legends

Unit 2: The Stone Age

New Words

ice age   midden   hunter-gatherers   nomad   flint   sinew   vessel   settlement   ancient
winter solstice   chieftain

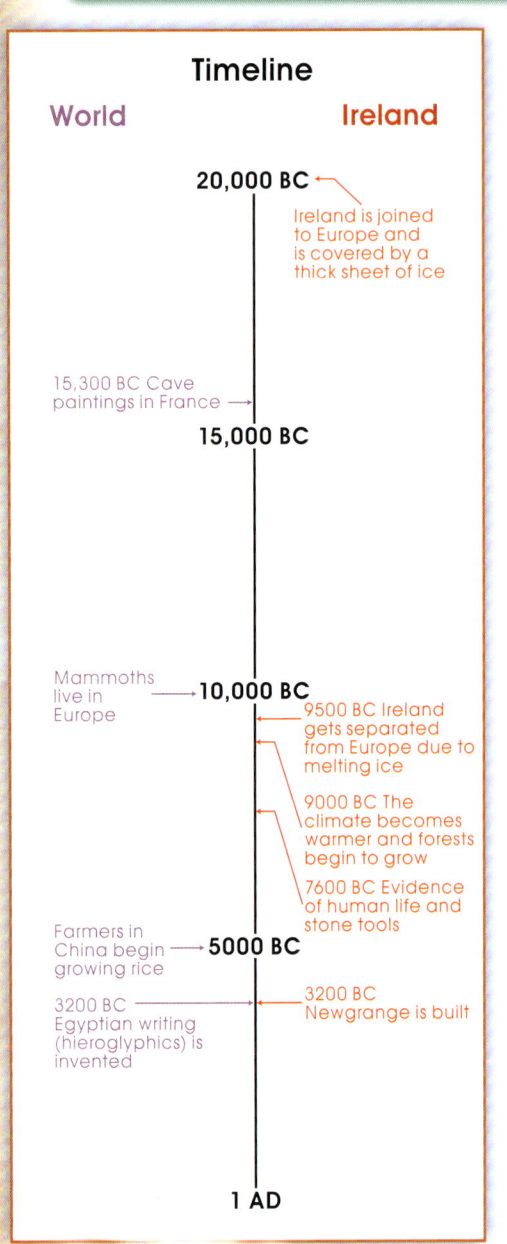

Timeline

World		Ireland
	20,000 BC	Ireland is joined to Europe and is covered by a thick sheet of ice
15,300 BC Cave paintings in France	15,000 BC	
Mammoths live in Europe	10,000 BC	9500 BC Ireland gets separated from Europe due to melting ice
		9000 BC The climate becomes warmer and forests begin to grow
		7600 BC Evidence of human life and stone tools
Farmers in China begin growing rice	5000 BC	
3200 BC Egyptian writing (hieroglyphics) is invented		3200 BC Newgrange is built
	1 AD	

Stone Age people come to Ireland

The first people who came to Ireland crossed over from Britain at the end of the last ice age. This was around the year 8000 BC. At that time, there were certain places between Ireland and Britain where the sea was quite shallow. The people may have walked across to Ireland or else rowed across in boats made from hollowed-out tree trunks. They found a land with lots of plants and forests of birch, hazel, elm and oak trees.

Animals such as wild boar, hares and elks (a huge type of deer that is now extinct here) roamed freely. The rivers were full of trout, salmon and eels. When we look at the remains of the graves and the tools that were left by these people, we begin to get a picture of how they lived. Their middens (rubbish tips) have been found to contain animal bones, sea shells and fruit seeds. This gives us information about their diet.

Hot History
The Earth has had four periods of very cold weather known as ice ages.

Hot History
We use the letters, 'BC', to tell us when times like the Stone Age took place. 'BC' means before the birth of Christ. Something that happened 8000 years before Christ is written as '8000 BC'.

Strand: Early People and Ancient Societies   Strand Unit: Stone Age Peoples

Food

The Stone Age people are known as 'hunter-gatherers'. They lived by hunting wild beasts, catching fish and gathering nuts and berries. They were also nomads, meaning that they moved from place to place to follow the supply of food. They lived in caves or beside a river that supplied them with fish. They could also travel up and down the river in their boats. Those who lived beside the sea hunted seals and dolphins and collected shellfish. They also hunted birds and collected their eggs.

When they wanted to cook something, the Stone Age people dug a pit in the ground. They lined the pit with waterproof animal skins and then filled up the pit with water. After that, they cleaned out the stomach of a dead animal and filled it with meat, herbs, roots and nuts. The stomach was then tied up tightly. In the meantime, the water in the pit had been boiled up by adding red-hot stones from the nearby fire. The stomach was then placed into the boiling water. As it cooked, all the flavours of the food blended together. Mmm!

Hot History

Stone Age people in Europe hunted mammoths for food. A mammoth looked like a large, red, hairy elephant.

Cooking in a pit

Tools and weapons

Nothing was wasted by the hunter-gatherers. They used the meat of animals for food, the skins to make clothes and shelters, the fat to light lamps and the bones to make tools like sewing needles, knives and skin scrapers. Even their jewellery was made from the bones and teeth of animals! They also used a hard stone called flint to make tools and weapons. Hammers made from bone were used to shape the flint stones into razor-sharp axes and knives. Sinews (the tough tissues that join muscle to bone) were used to tie the flint or bone blades to wooden handles in order to make weapons.

Hot History

It could be chilly in Stone Age times, so people rubbed animal fat onto their skin to keep out the cold. Imagine that for perfume!

Strand: Early People and Ancient Societies   Strand Unit: Stone Age Peoples

ACTIVITIES

1. Use the following words to write about the Stone Age people.
   (a) ice age, (b) Britain, (c) nomads, (d) flint
2. Draw and label a list of things that you might find in a Stone Age midden.
3. Pair work: *Stone Age people were physically strong, but they were not very clever.* Do you agree or disagree? Talk about it first and then write your answer.

Hunter-gatherers became farmers

Clearing the land

The hunter-gatherer way of life continued in Ireland until about 4000 BC. After that, although people still used their stone weapons to hunt animals, they also began to learn about farming. They began to use axes to clear woodland so that they could grow wheat and barley. They also burned the land to clear it of tree stumps and bushes. They used these cleared areas as grazing land for their cattle, sheep, pigs and goats. All of those animals were once living in the forests. The first farmers had to catch and tame animals such as wild pigs.

Stone Age people no longer needed to be nomads. They could keep their animals nearby and build homes that would last. They also made some great discoveries such as how to make pottery from clay. The pots were very handy, as they could be used for storing food. They could also be used as lamps. They filled a pot with a small amount of animal fat and then lit the fat. Hey presto, a lamp! Clay pots, also known as food vessels, were filled with goodies and buried with the dead.

Hot History

Bet you didn't know that Stone Age people had disposable nappies! Moss was used to keep babies dry. It was held in place by animal skins. The moss soaked up the wetness, meaning dry babies' bottoms!

Stone Age grave

Strand: Early People and Ancient Societies   Strand Unit: Stone Age Peoples

Stone Age builders

Stone Age people were very good builders. We can see this in the remains of their buildings, tombs and monuments around the country. There is evidence of a farming settlement at the Céide Fields in County Mayo. A settlement is a community with homes built close to each other. Very old, or ancient, fields surrounded by stone walls have been found at the Céide Fields. A Stone Age house was rectangular in shape. It could be made from branches woven together and covered with mud, or from tree trunks that were sunk straight down into the ground. A small hole in the roof allowed smoke to escape.

Stone Age house

Newgrange

The most exciting building was found at Newgrange, County Meath. Newgrange is an amazing tomb or temple, which looks like a cathedral. Chieftains may have been buried at Newgrange. There are a number of standing stones there that may have been used to mark their graves.

Newgrange

The seasons were very important to Stone Age people, as they needed fine weather for their crops to grow. The sun and the spirit world were also of great importance in their lives. Because of all these things, they took great care when building the tomb at Newgrange. Huge boulders were hauled there, from as far away as Wicklow and Drogheda. Can you imagine how difficult it was to do that without the use of lorries and machinery, or even a horse and cart? However, Stone Age people were very good at solving problems. They placed the huge stones on top of strong tree trunks. The trunks rolled along beneath the stones, making it much easier to bring the massive stones from one place to another.

Moving the stones

Strand: Early People and Ancient Societies   Strand Unit: Stone Age Peoples

Stone Age Beliefs

Stone Age people believed that the worlds of the living and of the dead were linked. The great tomb at Newgrange was built as a symbol of this belief, for everyone to see. Stone Age people who were interested in the stars and planets figured out that December 21st was the shortest day of the year. This day is known as the winter solstice. The burial chamber at the centre of Newgrange was built in such a way that, when the sun rises on December 21st, it shines directly onto the place where a dead person would have lain. More than 5000 years later, people visit Newgrange every year to see the sun lighting up the burial chamber.

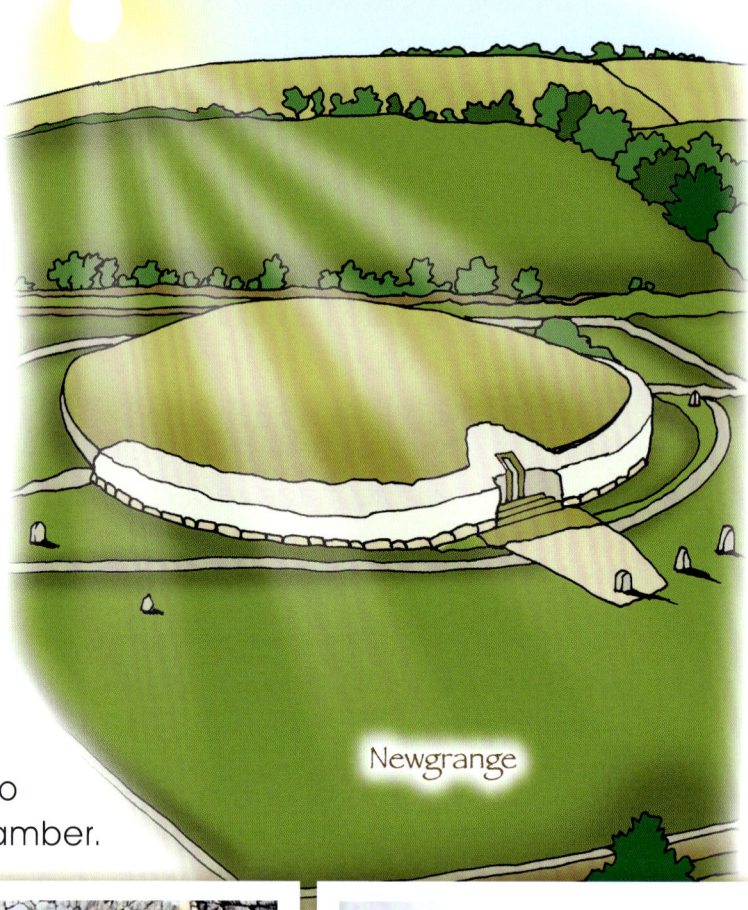

Newgrange

Sun shining through the passage at Newgrange on December 21st

Beautiful spiral carvings on the boulders at Newgrange

One of the standing stones at Newgrange

Strand: Early People and Ancient Societies Strand Unit: Stone Age Peoples

ACTIVITIES

A. Can You Remember?

1. When did the first Stone Age people come to Ireland and how did they get here?
2. What kind of food was eaten by Stone Age people?
3. What were Stone Age tools made from?
4. Why were the seasons important to Stone Age people?
5. Name one discovery made by Stone Age people.

B. Choose the Correct Answer to Complete Each Sentence.

1. A mammoth was a type of _____.
   A. elk, **B.** pig, **C.** elephant, or **D.** sheep
2. Cave paintings were found in _____.
   A. the Céide Fields, **B.** County Meath, **C.** France, or **D.** Newgrange
3. The elk is a type of _____.
   A. bear, **B.** dog, **C.** fish, or **D.** deer
4. One weapon used by Stone Age people was _____.
   A. a longbow, **B.** an axe, **C.** a shield, or **D.** a sword

C. Think About It.

1. Why do you think it was important for Stone Age farmers to build settlements?
2. Why do you think it was important that the sun would shine onto the place where a dead person would have lain at Newgrange?
3. Why do you think the Stone Age people buried food vessels with the dead?

D. Get Creative.

1. Imagine that you have gone back to Stone Age times for a week. Write a diary describing what it is like to live by hunting, fishing and gathering your food.
2. Practise drawing single, double and triple spirals on a page using different colour crayons. Next, colour the whole page with a black crayon. Use the end of a pencil or a spoon to scrape out a spiral design through the black colour.
3. Do you think that Stone Age people would like the way that Ireland has changed? List three changes they would be happy with and three that might upset them.

E. Digging Deeper

1. Watch the film, *The Mummy*, to get an idea of how ancient people used burial chambers for their dead.
2. Use the internet to find out lots more about the Stone Age. Your teacher will give you a list of words to key into a search engine.

Strand: Early People and Ancient Societies   Strand Unit: Stone Age Peoples

Unit 3: Food and Farming

New Words

yoke   combine harvester   quern-stone   archaeologist   blight   organic   domesticated   billycan
free range   battery

Timeline

World | **Ireland**

- Beginning of the Middle Ages → 500 AD
- 1000 AD
- End of the Middle Ages → 1500 AD
- 1589 AD The potato comes to Ireland
- 1766 AD The turkey is brought to Europe from America
- 1766 AD The world's first fizzy drink is made in Trinity College Dublin
- 1845 AD Great Famine hits Ireland
- 1862 AD Louis Pasteur discovers how to make food safe to eat
- 1933 AD Cadbury's Chocolate Factory opens in Dublin
- 2000 AD

Cereal Crops

We know from looking at the contents of Bronze Age middens, that cereal crops like wheat and barley have been grown in Ireland for thousands of years. These crops are still grown and eaten all around the world, but the way in which they are grown now is quite different to the way they were grown in the past. Cereal crops must be planted, looked after and then harvested in autumn. Their grains are used to make our breakfast cereals, bread and pasta. The early farmers used wooden spades and ploughs to prepare the land for planting. A wooden yoke that dates from the Bronze Age tells us that horses or oxen may have pulled the ploughs then. Today, most farmers use a tractor to do this work.

Hot History

The Bronze Age began in Ireland about 2000 BC. The Bronze Age yoke rested on the necks of two oxen so that they would pull the plough together – like in this photo.

Horse-drawn plough

Tractor-drawn plough

Wheat  → Grain  → Flour  → Bread

Strand: Continuity and Change Over Time   Strand Unit: Food and Farming

When crops have grown and they are ready to be harvested, they must be cut and gathered. The grains must be separated from the stems. Machines called combine harvesters do all of this work now. This is very different from the way crops were gathered in the past. Bronze Age farmers used a scythe or a team of horses to do the harvesting. When the grain was gathered, it had to be ground using quern-stones. In later times, wheat and barley were brought to the mill, where huge millstones crushed the grain and turned it into flour. Instead of paying for this service with money, people often paid the miller by giving him some of the flour.

Team of horses harvesting crops

Scythe

Combine harvester

Barley and wheat

For poor people in the Middle Ages (500-1500 AD), barley was a very important cereal. In fact, they ate it for breakfast, lunch and dinner. They used barley to make porridge and pancakes. They also had barley soup and barley bread. They tried to make their meals a bit more interesting by adding carrots or cabbage and onions or garlic. For dessert, they had home-made cheese and wild apples sweetened with honey. The food that was eaten by rich people was more exciting. They could afford wheat, which made their bread taste nicer. They also had roast beef, pork, lamb chops, rabbits, poultry and eggs.

Maize

Archaeologists have found evidence that Mexicans began growing maize about 10,000 years ago. Maize is the main food eaten in many countries, including South Africa and Brazil. Often it is still harvested by hand in those places – just like when it was first grown. In wealthy countries like the USA, machines are used to do this work. Tortilla chips and taco shells are made from maize.

Maize

Hot History

Quern-stones were stone tools that were used to grind things like grain. The stones were used in pairs. The lower stone was called a quern, while the upper stone was called a handstone.

Hot History

In the past, there were no fridges or freezers to keep food fresh. Meat and fish were dried, salted or pickled in vinegar so that they would not rot. Butter was kept in cold water to stop it from melting.

Strand: Continuity and Change Over Time   Strand Unit: Food and Farming

IRELAND AND THE POTATO CROP

About 150 years ago, the potato was the main food eaten by most people in Ireland. In fact, many poor people had nothing else to eat except a certain type of potato called a 'Lumper'. In the 1840s, the potato crop was attacked by a disease called 'blight'. Blight caused the potatoes to rot in the ground. The Great Famine, as it is called, had a serious effect on the people of Ireland. More than a million people died of hunger and another million left Ireland to live in foreign countries. During that time, some artists drew pictures of what was happening in Ireland. The pictures help us to understand what life was like for people during the Great Famine. Potatoes are still an important food in our country and we eat them boiled, roasted or chipped.

Emigrants Leave Ireland by Henry Doyle

Skibbereen 1847 by James Mahony

Hot History

Potatoes were first grown in the Andes Mountains in South America. They were brought to Ireland by Sir Walter Raleigh in 1589.

THE OLD AND THE NEW

The Roman Emperor Tiberius was the first person to think of helping plants to grow in a warm place. He wanted a fresh cucumber on his dinner plate every day of the year. His gardeners went to great trouble to make sure that the cucumbers were not damaged by cold and frost. Today, greenhouses allow farmers in Ireland to grow foods like tomatoes and courgettes that would not have grown well here in the past.

Crops growing in a greenhouse

The early farmers used animal manure to make the soil better for growing plants. Today, some farmers use chemicals to help plants to grow. Sometimes they use sprays to kill pests that might damage the crop. People who grow food in an organic way prefer to use natural products such as manure instead of chemicals and sprays. They use insects like ladybirds to eat the pests that destroy plants.

Strand: Continuity and Change Over Time   Strand Unit: Food and Farming

ACTIVITIES

1. Match the words in column A with the definitions in column B.

A	B
planting	• a large, sharp tool used for cutting crops
harvesting	• a machine used to separate grains from stems
cereals	• a disease that affects the potato
yoke	• a beam used between two horses or oxen to help them pull together
scythe	• farming activity carried out in spring
combine harvester	• grain crops
blight	• farming activity carried out in autumn

2. Group work: *Farming is not as important today as it was in the past.* Do you agree or disagree with this sentence? Talk about it and then write your answer.

3. Think of some foods that you have for breakfast, for example, porridge, corn flakes and shredded wheat. Can you name the cereals from which they are made?

Farm animals

There is evidence that cattle, sheep, goats and pigs were reared on Bronze Age farms. There have been lots of changes since then in the way that our food is produced, but a lot of the old ways are still in use today – especially by organic farmers.

Cattle

Cattle have always been popular farm animals, because they give us meat (beef) and milk. The burgers, steaks and roasts we like to eat are most often made from beef. Cattle in Ireland are usually reared on farms where they have plenty of fresh grass to eat. Dairy cows produce lots of milk, which gives us products like butter, cheese and yoghurt. When cows became tame, or domesticated, the early farmers learned to milk them by hand. Some farmers still do this, but most cows are now milked by machines. In the past, people bought milk in jugs or open cans called 'billycans' from the dairyman. After that, milk was sold in glass bottles. The lids of the bottles were made from tinfoil. The milkman came early in the morning and left the milk on the doorstep. Clever birds sometimes pecked through the lids in order to sip the cream that would rise to the top of the milk. Today, we buy our milk in cartons or plastic containers.

Milking by hand

Milking with a machine

Sheep

Sheep have always been valued for their meat and wool. Sheep are shorn in late spring and early summer. In the past, the sheep shearer used a huge pair of scissors, or clippers, to cut off the sheep's fleece. Today, electric clippers are used by most shearers.

Shearing with clippers

Pigs

People in Ireland and all across Northern Europe have bred pigs for thousands of years, because they provide us with such tasty food. They give us a great variety of meat, like sausages, rashers, pork and ham. In the past, pigs were kept in pens or fields. Most Irish farmers killed at least one pig each year to provide meat for the family. Every part of the pig was used in some way. Men and women each had different tasks. Men killed, cleaned, butchered and salted, while women cooked the pig's feet (also known as trotters or 'crubeens') and made black pudding. This involved mixing pig blood with oatmeal, fat, herbs, salt and pepper. The mixture was poured into long lengths of the pig's insides, which were put into a big pot and boiled. Ham was made by smoking the meat over a turf fire. It was then hung from the rafters. The turf smoke gave the meat a lovely flavour.

Smoking the ham

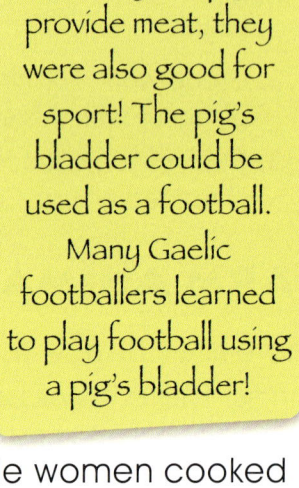

Hot History

Not only did pigs provide meat, they were also good for sport! The pig's bladder could be used as a football. Many Gaelic footballers learned to play football using a pig's bladder!

Poultry

The way poultry (chickens, ducks, geese and turkeys) is kept has also changed over time. Chickens love to peck around in the earth for worms and seeds. Some of them still do and they are called 'free range' chickens. Some poultry farms keep thousands of chickens that are housed indoors. They are fed and watered automatically and are known as battery chickens. The word 'battery' means a 'group of'.

Battery Chickens

Strand: Continuity and Change Over Time | Strand Unit: Food and Farming

ACTIVITIES

A. Can You Remember?

1. What did the early farmers use to prepare the ground for planting?
2. (a) When did the Great Famine happen in Ireland? (b) What effect did it have?
3. Where was maize first grown?
4. (a) From which animal do we get ham? (b) How was it made in the past?
5. What was the name of the Roman Emperor who liked to eat cucumbers?

B. Choose the Correct Answer to Complete Each Sentence.

1. The Great Famine happened in _____.
   A. the 1840s, B. the 1480s, C. 1800, or D. 1980
2. Tame or domesticated animals include _____.
   A. foxes, B. cattle, C. wolves, or D. tigers
3. Dairy products are made from _____.
   A. beef, B. milk, C. maize, or D. ham
4. During the Great Famine, about _____ people died from hunger.
   A. 1000, B. 10,000, C. 100, or D. 1 million

C. Think About It.

1. Why do you think machines are used for farming in some countries, while the work is done by hand in others?
2. Find out from your parents and/or grandparents what kinds of food they had for breakfast and dinner when they were children. (a) Make a list of those foods and compare them with what you eat today. (b) Was there more or less choice in the past?

D. Get Creative.

1. Write out a weekly dinner menu for the Middle Ages for (a) poor people and (b) wealthy people. (c) Write out a weekly dinner menu for yourself.
2. You are an artist living in Ireland during the Great Famine. Draw a scene to show people around the world what was happening in Ireland at that time.
3. How can we make sure that everyone in the world has enough to eat? Write a speech describing how rich countries can help poor farmers around the world.

E. Digging Deeper

1. Read the novel, *The Long March* by Marie-Louise Fitzpatrick (Random House), to learn how the Choktaw Native American tribe helped Irish people during the Great Famine.
2. Read the book, *The Táin* by Liam Mac Uistin (O'Brien Press), to find out about the legend of Queen Méabh and the Brown Bull of Cooley.

Strand: Continuity and Change Over Time   Strand Unit: Food and Farming

Unit 4: People of the Tigris and Euphrates Rivers

New Words

Mesopotamia   fertile   silt   loam   Sumerians   Akkadians   reservoir   irrigation   ziggurat
cuneiform   tablet   charcoal   bronze   smith

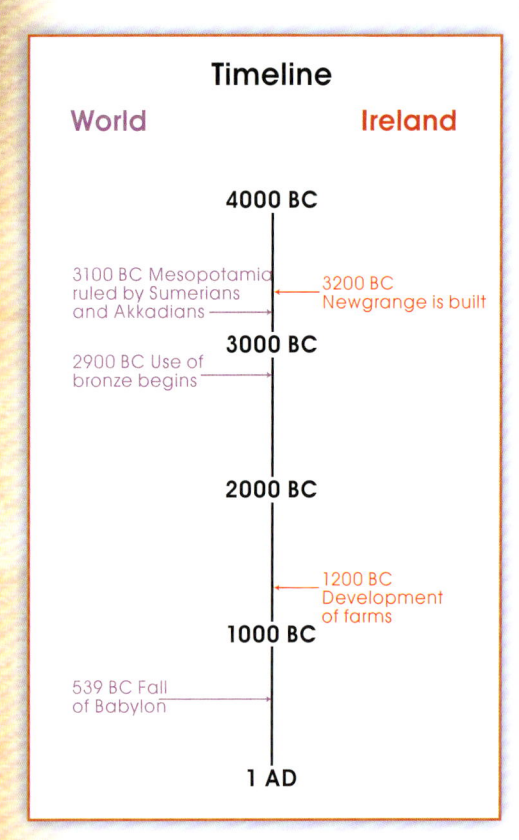

Timeline

World | **Ireland**

- 4000 BC
- 3100 BC Mesopotamia ruled by Sumerians and Akkadians
- 3200 BC Newgrange is built
- 3000 BC
- 2900 BC Use of bronze begins
- 2000 BC
- 1200 BC Development of farms
- 1000 BC
- 539 BC Fall of Babylon
- 1 AD

The Tigris and the Euphrates

The Tigris and the Euphrates are two very important rivers. Almost 7000 years ago, people began to settle in the area between the two rivers. The area became known as Mesopotamia. The word 'Mesopotamia' means the 'land between two rivers': the Tigris and the Euphrates. This area lies in the country that is now called Iraq. The soil in the land between the two rivers was very good for growing crops. We call this kind of soil 'fertile'. The soil was fertile because of the build up of a mixture of sand, clay (fine soil) and silt (grainy soil), which together formed loam. Loam is a great soil for growing plants. Almost every year, the two rivers flooded and burst their banks. The silt from the rivers was left behind, turning the land into a swamp. When the swamp dried out, the land was very good for farming. This area of land became known as the 'Fertile Crescent'.

Euphrates

Strand: Early People and Ancient Societies   **Strand Unit:** Early Societies of the Tigris and Euphrates Valleys

Farming

The upper part of Mesopotamia was called Akkad and the people who lived there were the Akkadians. Sumer was the name of the lower part of Mesopotamia and the people who lived there were the Sumerians. The Sumerians are the people we will be learning about. The Sumerians kept cattle, goats and sheep and they built huts from reeds. They built huge banks to stop the two rivers from flooding their farms. They also built canals, dams and reservoirs. A reservoir stores water. It is a huge lake made by people. The dams and canals helped the Sumerians to guide the water to where it was needed. This process is called irrigation. They lived by farming, fishing and hunting wild birds. They grew crops like barley, wheat, dates and vegetables. As farming improved, the Sumerians became rich and their villages grew into towns and cities. By 3500 BC, Sumer had large, wealthy cities such as Ur, which was home to 24,000 people. Each Sumerian city had its own irrigation system for the surrounding land.

Sumerian irrigation

Trade

One of the most important inventions was the wheel. The invention of the wheel and the plough meant that farming improved. Oxen were used to pull carts and ploughs. Ploughing the fields with an ox-drawn plough was faster than ploughing by hand, so it took less time to get the fields ready for planting. This meant that two harvests could be produced in a year instead of just one. The extra crops could then be sold. The Sumerians traded their corn, dates, leather and wool with Syria and other neighbouring counties near the Persian Gulf and India. While selling their produce abroad, they bought goods like timber, metals and precious stones to bring back to Mesopotamia. Some people became experts at making tools and pottery, which were also traded for other goods.

Mesopotamian wheel

Sumerian pottery

Strand: Early People and Ancient Societies Strand Unit: Early Societies of the Tigris and Euphrates Valleys

23

Sumerian kings, gods and priests

Each Sumerian city had a king, who was responsible for ruling his city. He also had to make sure that the irrigation system surrounding the city was kept running properly. Sumerian cities had walls around them. At the centre of each city was a temple, which the people believed was home to a god. The Sumerians believed that humans were created to supply the gods with food, drink and shelter. They worshipped many gods and each city had its own god. The temple provided the god with shelter and the priests collected taxes from the people to pay for the god's food and drink. The temple was built on the top of a high tower called a 'ziggurat'. The ziggurat was built on a rectangular, an oval or a square platform. It was built mostly from sun-baked bricks. There were between two and seven levels in the ziggurat, with the temple on the top level. The temple could be reached by walking up a ramp.

The Great Ziggurat of Ur, Mesopotamia

Writing and learning

The Sumerians were very clever and they were the first people to work out how to add, subtract and multiply. Our basic unit in mathematics is 10, but the Sumerian basic unit was 60. Our system of having 60 minutes in an hour and 360 degrees in a circle comes from the Sumerians. They worked out a calendar based on the cycle of the moon, with a year of 12 months. They were also the first people to learn how to write. The priests wanted to write because they needed to keep a record of all the taxes they collected. They began to write by drawing pictures of the things that they wished to explain or record. For example, they drew a cow's head with a number of dots or circles to show the number of cows they were talking about.

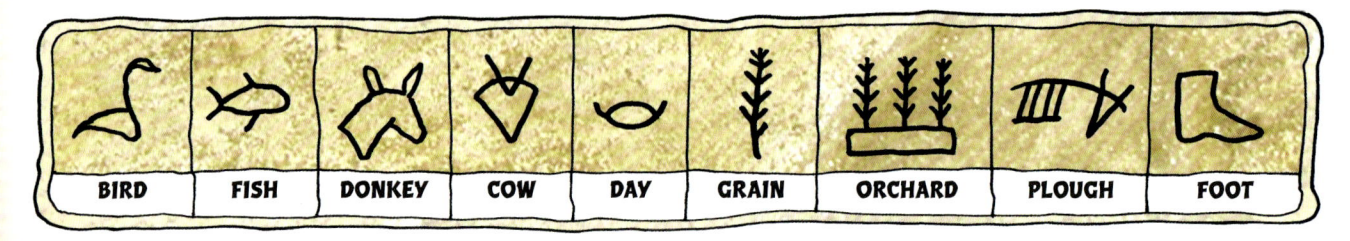

Sumerian writing with pictures

| BIRD | FISH | DONKEY | COW | DAY | GRAIN | ORCHARD | PLOUGH | FOOT |

Examples of Sumerian pictures and their meanings

Strand: Early People and Ancient Societies   Strand Unit: Early Societies of the Tigris and Euphrates Valleys

Cuneiform writing

Later on, the Sumerians wrote by making patterns instead of pictures. This kind of writing is called cuneiform writing. They used V-shaped sticks or reeds to make the patterns on a block, or tablet, of wet clay. The wet clay tablet was then baked in an oven until it was hard. The Sumerians even wrote down some of their myths and legends on clay tablets and some of these have survived until the present day.

Cuneiform writing

Writing on a tablet

Discovery of bronze

The Sumerians discovered how to get copper from rock by using charcoal to heat the rock. Around 2900 BC, they realised that copper could be made stronger by adding tin. The mixture of tin and copper produced a new material. The new material, bronze, was much harder and stronger than either copper or tin. Bronze objects such as ornaments, tools, vases and weapons have been found at the Sumerian city of Ur. Bronze weapons were better than stone weapons and the people who used them became very powerful. Bronze tools made life easier for farmers. Wheels were made lighter and stronger by using bronze spokes instead of pieces of wood. A strip of bronze on the rim of the wheel helped to keep the spokes in place.

Sumerian bronze ornament

Hot History

A person who makes objects from metal is known as a smith. Smiths often keep their methods secret!

Strand: Early People and Ancient Societies   Strand Unit: Early Societies of the Tigris and Euphrates Valleys

Babylon

The city of Babylon in Mesopotamia was one of the great cities of the Ancient World. It was built on the River Euphrates, about 80 km south of the modern city of Baghdad, in Iraq. Babylon was a very wealthy city and the Hanging Gardens in the Palace at Babylon were one of the Seven Wonders of the Ancient World. The city was founded around 2300 BC and it was the main city in the powerful empire of Babylonia.

Hanging Gardens of Babylon

Discovery at Ur

Jewellery from the Royal Tombs of Ur

In 1929, a number of Royal Tombs were discovered at the city of Ur. People were amazed to find glittering treasures made by the Bronze Age smiths of Ur. Helmets, swords, spears and knives were all found in the graves. Abargi, the King of Ur, ruled the city almost 5000 years ago. When he died, his body was dressed in fine clothes and placed on a cart pulled by two oxen. The cart was driven to a grave, where the king's body was then laid out. All of his weapons and riches were spread out around him. More than 60 people agreed to die with him, so that they could serve their king in the next life. The women who died wore precious earrings and necklaces. The men had spears and knives in their hands. However, Mesopotamia was the first known area where a group of people managed to live closely and peacefully together.

Ox-drawn cart bringing the King of Ur to his grave

ACTIVITIES

A. Can You Remember?

1. What is the name of the area that lay between the River Tigris and the River Euphrates?
2. Who were the people who lived in this area?
3. Why did the Sumerians build canals?
4. About how many people lived in the city of Ur?
5. Who collected taxes in Sumeria?

B. Choose the Correct Answer to Complete Each Sentence.

1. Mesopotamia lay _____ the River Tigris and River Euphrates.
   A. above, B. beside, C. between, or D. under
2. The king of a city was in charge of _____.
   A. the irrigation system, B. the wheels, C. the walls, or D. writing
3. The Sumerians were the first people to learn to _____.
   A. type, B. sing, C. dance, or D. write
4. Cuneiform writing was made up of _____.
   A. patterns, B. letters, C. numbers, or D. dots

C. Think About It.

1. What words would you use to describe the Sumerians?
2. Why do you think Babylon was such an important city?
3. Why do you think we no longer use cuneiform writing?
4. Why was the invention of the wheel so important?

D. Get Creative.

1. Explain the word 'irrigation' to someone who has never heard of it.
2. (a) Write this message using pictures only: *A boat was in a storm for seven nights and seven days.*
   (b) Write a message for your friend using pictures only. Can she or he read it?
3. You are a servant of the King of Ur. Now that he has died, you are supposed to go with him to his grave! What will you do?
4. Write a fact file about the Sumerians. Choose your own headings.

E. Digging Deeper

1. Read the book, *Ancient World* by Fiona Chandler (Usborne World History).
2. Use the internet to find out interesting facts about Mesopotamia. Your teacher will give you a list of words to key into a search engine.

Strand: Early People and Ancient Societies   Strand Unit: Early Societies of the Tigris and Euphrates Valleys

Unit 5: Setanta

New Words
sliotar   Macra   blacksmith   banquet   wolfhound

1

Long, long ago, Conor MacNessa was the King of Ulster. He lived in his palace at Eamhain Macha with a special band of warriors, known as the 'Red Branch Knights'. The knights were very strong and brave. Boys who wanted to become members of the Red Branch Knights had to join the Macra first. They learned how to fight and use weapons while they were in the Macra.

2

King Conor had a nephew called Setanta, who lived with his mother near Dundalk in County Louth. Setanta wanted to join the Macra. When he was nine years old, he set off towards his uncle's palace. He took his hurley, a sliotar, a small sword and a spear with him. As he walked along the path, he stopped every so often to hit the sliotar with his hurley. Then he ran to catch the sliotar before it hit the ground!

3

When he reached his uncle's palace at Eamhain Macha, Setanta saw the boys of the Macra playing hurling. Setanta loved hurling so much that he ran over and joined the game. He was much stronger than the other boys and he scored lots of goals. The boys were angry and they started to fight with Setanta, but he was able to defend himself.

Hot History

The Poc Fada Hurling and Camogie Championship is held in the Cooley Mountains in County Louth every year. It is held to honour Setanta's great ability as a hurler. Go to www.gaa.ie to find out more.

Strand: Story   Strand Unit: Myths and Legends

4

"YOU'VE GROWN SO BIG! YOU'RE STRONG AND BRAVE, TOO, SO YOU MUST JOIN THE MACRA."

"I AM SETANTA, YOUR NEPHEW."

King Conor saw what was happening and he wanted to know more about the new boy. He ordered for the boy to be brought before him, so that he could ask him where he had come from.

5

"I WOULD LOVE TO JOIN THE MACRA, UNCLE CONOR. I HOPE TO BECOME A RED BRANCH KNIGHT."

King Conor made peace between Setanta and the other boys and Setanta joined the Macra.

6

At that time, a famous blacksmith called Culann worked for King Conor. Culann was a skilled craftsman, who made swords, spears and other weapons. King Conor and his friends were invited to Culann's house for a banquet. Setanta was also invited, but he said that he wanted to finish a game of hurling first.

7

"HAS EVERYONE ARRIVED?"

"YES, THEY'RE ALL HERE."

When King Conor and his friends arrived, Culann welcomed them and led them into the banqueting hall. The king completely forgot about Setanta.

Strand: Story   Strand Unit: Myths and Legends

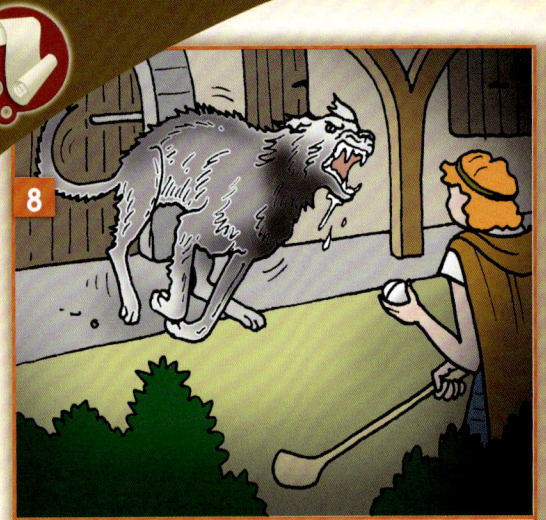

8 Culann's watchdog was a fierce wolfhound with huge jaws and big, sharp teeth. Culann put the hound on guard and he closed the doors. Setanta arrived shortly afterwards, carrying his sliotar and hurley. As soon as the hound saw Setanta, it charged at him with its mouth wide open.

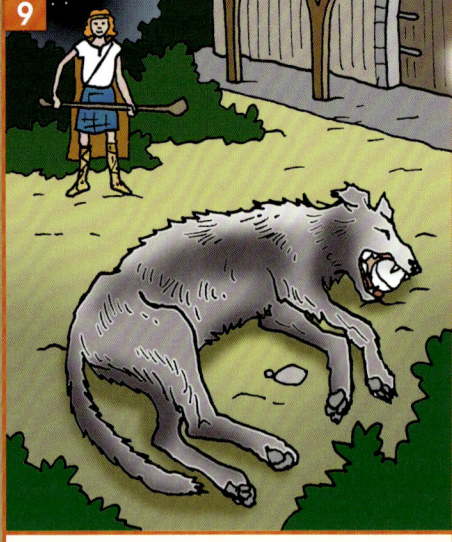

9 Quick as a flash, Setanta hit the sliotar with a mighty blow of his hurley. He sent it straight into the open mouth of the hound. Culann's great dog fell dead on the ground.

Hot History

The Irish wolfhound is one of the tallest dogs in the world. It grows to about 80 cm in height. It was used in Ireland long ago for hunting wolves, deer and other wild animals.

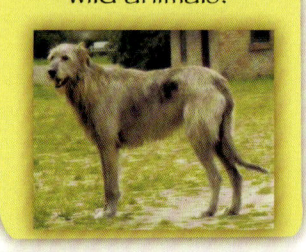

10 When the people at the feast heard the noise, they rushed outside to see what had happened. King Conor and his friends were delighted to see that Setanta was safe, but Culann was very upset.

> WHO WILL GUARD MY HOUSE NOW?

> I WILL DO IT UNTIL YOU FIND ANOTHER GUARD DOG AS GOOD AS THE ONE I HAVE KILLED.

11 Setanta was given the name 'Cúchulainn', which means the 'hound of Culann'. He became a Red Branch Knight. When Connacht and Ulster were at war, Cúchulainn was the only warrior left to defend Ulster. The other knights were in a deep sleep due to a magician's spell. Cúchulainn fought alone and he became the greatest warrior in Ulster.

Strand: Story **Strand Unit:** Myths and Legends

ACTIVITIES

A. Can You Remember?

1. Who was Setanta's uncle?
2. Why did Setanta want to join the Macra?
3. Who were the Red Branch Knights?
4. Why were all the people in Culann's house?
5. What is the Poc Fada?

B. Choose the Correct Answer to Complete Each Sentence.

1. Culann was a famous _____.
   A. soldier, B. teacher, C. blacksmith, or D. hurler
2. The Irish Wolfhound was used to hunt _____.
   A. deer, B. rats, C. cattle, or D. sheep
3. Setanta killed the hound with a _____.
   A. sliotar, B. football, C. sword, or D. spear
4. Cúchulainn was the only warrior left to defend _____.
   A. Munster, B. Ulster, C. Leinster, or D. Louth

C. Think About It.

1. Why do you think Setanta hit the ball and then ran to catch it as he walked along?
2. Do you think Setanta was right to join the game of hurling without being asked? Give a reason for your answer.
3. Do you think Setanta had to kill the wolfhound?
4. What do you think Culann said to Setanta after the hound was killed? Write the conversation between the two of them.

D. Get Creative.

1. Write a radio commentary for the match in which Setanta took part without being asked.
2. Imagine that you are Setanta. Write a diary page about your journey to Eamhain Macha. Describe how you felt when you met King Conor.
3. Debate the topic: *Girls should have been allowed to join the Macra*. Write down your points and ideas first.

E. Digging Deeper

1. Read the book, *The Hound of Ulster* by Malachy Doyle (A & C Black).
2. Look back to Unit 1. Compare Setanta with Fionn. In what way are they similar? In what way are they different?

Strand: Story   Strand Unit: Myths and Legends

Unit 6: Games and Pastimes

New Words

Colosseum   gladiator   mummers   falconry

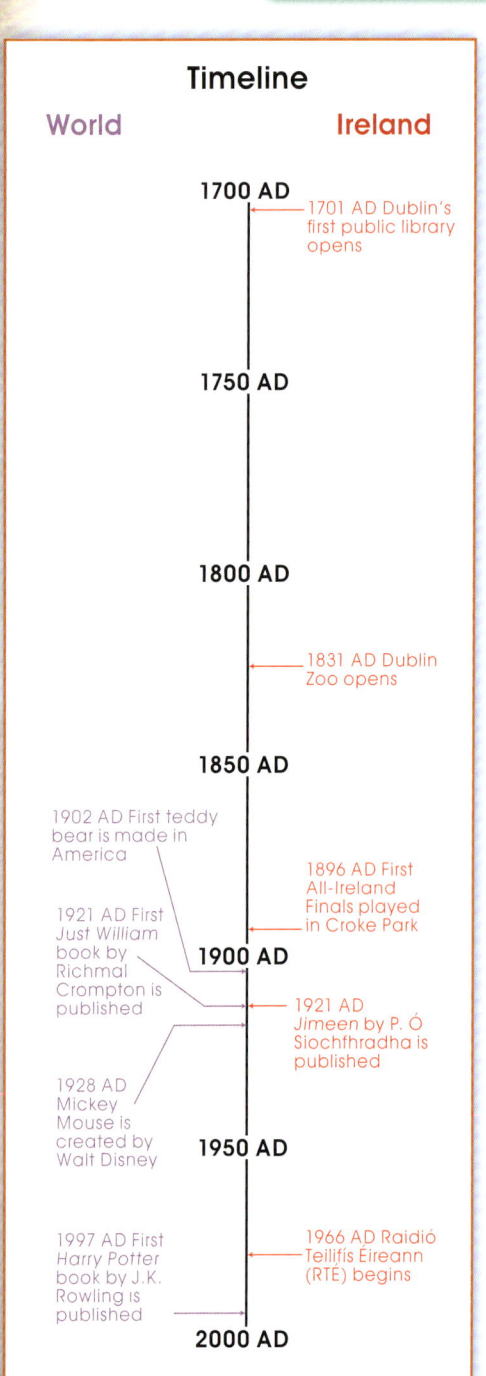

Timeline

World — **Ireland**

- 1700 AD
- 1701 AD Dublin's first public library opens
- 1750 AD
- 1800 AD
- 1831 AD Dublin Zoo opens
- 1850 AD
- 1902 AD First teddy bear is made in America
- 1896 AD First All-Ireland Finals played in Croke Park
- 1921 AD First *Just William* book by Richmal Crompton is published
- 1900 AD
- 1921 AD *Jimeen* by P. Ó Siochfhradha is published
- 1928 AD Mickey Mouse is created by Walt Disney
- 1950 AD
- 1966 AD Raidió Teilifís Éireann (RTÉ) begins
- 1997 AD First *Harry Potter* book by J.K. Rowling is published
- 2000 AD

Games of Ancient Greece

Keeping fit and playing sport were very important in Ancient Greece (3000-450 BC). People believed that if you kept fit, you would have a healthy body and a healthy mind, even when you were very old. Sport was so popular with the people of Ancient Greece that they started the Olympic Games in a town called Olympia. The Olympic Games are still very important in the world of sport. They take place every four years and they are always held in a city. In 2012, the Olympic Games were held in London, England.

Olympic Medal Ceremony

Roman Entertainment

Games and competitions were also very popular in Ancient Rome (509 BC-476 AD). They were a lot more violent than those in Ancient Greece. The games took place in the Colosseum, which was like a football stadium. Instead of footballers, there were strong men known as gladiators, who fought against each other and against animals such as lions and tigers. Usually they fought until one of them was killed. For the Romans, the contests were a great day out. They bought treats on the way to the Colosseum and they clapped and cheered as a poor gladiator or animal was killed.

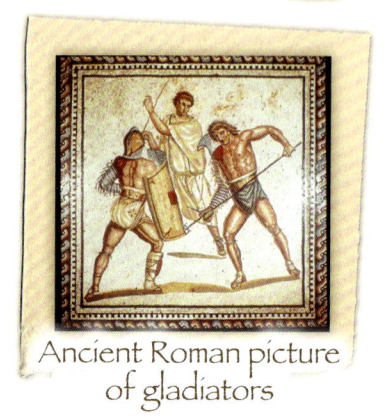

Colosseum

Ancient Roman picture of gladiators

Strand: Local Studies   Strand Unit: Games and Pastimes in the Past

MEDIEVAL PASTIMES

Some medieval pastimes were also very cruel. Dog fights and bear baiting were common. However, there were nicer ways for people to have fun. Football was played using a pig's bladder for a ball. Storytelling was very popular. Adults and children loved the religious stories told by the monks and priests. Crowds would gather to watch 'miracle plays', which told stories from the lives of saints. Craftsmen such as carpenters, shoemakers and candlemakers were the actors. People also liked to play cards. In fact, the joker and the royal families on our playing cards are still shown wearing medieval clothes. At Christmas, groups of actors, or 'mummers', dressed up and sang songs based on stories and legends.

Rich people liked falconry, which involved training a falcon (a type of hawk) to hunt small animals.

Hot History

Bear baiting involved chaining a poor bear to a post. A group of dogs was forced to attack the bear and kill it by biting its throat.

Group of mummers

Falcon

ACTIVITIES

1. Match the words in column A with the explanations in column B.

A	B
gladiator	• a large stadium where contests took place
miracle play	• using a bird to hunt
mummer	• a play about a saint's life
falconry	• an actor
Colosseum	• a man who took part in fighting competitions

2. Do you think that people had better ways of enjoying themselves in the past than we do today? Give reasons for your answer.

GAMES IN THE 1900s

Early in the 1900s, some children had a lot of chores to do and they had little time to play. When they had some free time, they used the street as their playground. Hopscotch was a great game for playing outdoors. Children also loved playing marbles. Another game was played using a stick to roll a wooden hoop along the ground. The hoop could also be used for skipping. There were not many toys, so games like leapfrog, hide-and-seek and skipping were played a lot.

Hopscotch

Strand: Local Studies   Strand Unit: Games and Pastimes in the Past   33

Playing outdoors in the 1950s

The seasons influenced the games that children played in the 1950s. In autumn, they collected horse-chestnuts, threaded them onto strings and held 'conker' battles. In summer, they built dens and went fishing in rivers. There were more toys in the 1950s than ever before, but children really liked making their own toys. They made swords, guns and bows and arrows from sticks and branches. They used them to play games like Cowboys and Indians. In this game, children divided into two groups and pretended to have a war. Today, children play a similar game called Cops and Robbers. Boys and girls also pretended to be the characters from their favourite comics and television shows. In the 1950s, televisions were all in black and white.

Playing conkers

Ready, steady, go-cart!

One of the most exciting toys made by children in the 1950s was the go-cart. Go-carts were made by attaching two pairs of wheels to a wooden box that had once contained food. The boxes came from local shops and the wheels were usually taken from old prams. A piece of rope was attached to the front so that the driver could steer. Sometimes the only brakes were the driver's feet!

Go-carting

Playing indoors in the 1950s

In the evening, or when it rained, children played board games such as Ludo, Snakes and Ladders and Chess. Many children collected stamps and stickers, which they swapped and displayed in albums. They also spent hours building things with Meccano and Lego. They liked to read a lot, so they often visited the library, where they could borrow books for free. Comics like *Dandy*, *Beano*, *Sparky*, *Topper*, *Victor*, *Bunty* and *Judy* were popular, too. The sitting room, or parlour, was usually a quiet place, where the family sat around the fireplace and read.

Train built with Meccano

Hot History
Dolls and teddies were used for playing games of house, hospital and school.

34   Strand: Local Studies   Strand Unit: Games and Pastimes in the Past

ACTIVITIES

A. Can You Remember?

1. How often do the Olympic Games take place?
2. When did Dublin Zoo open? (Hint: Look at the timeline.)
3. How long is it since the first *Just William* book was published?
4. What things were used to build a go-cart?
5. Name three indoor games from the 1950s.

B. Choose the Correct Answer to Complete Each Sentence.

1. Mickey Mouse was created in _____.
   A. 1921, **B.** 1942, **C.** 1961, or **D.** 1928
2. The first teddy bear was made in _____.
   A. 1209, **B.** 2009, **C.** 1902, or **D.** 1912
3. The Colosseum is in _____.
   A. Athens, **B.** Greece, **C.** Dublin, or **D.** Rome
4. Conkers come from the _____ tree.
   A. oak, **B.** horse chestnut, **C.** ash, or **D.** sycamore

C. Think About It.

1. Have a class debate on the topic: *Playing outside makes children healthy*.
2. Pair work: Should children's pastimes be chosen by parents and teachers or should children be free to choose for themselves? Talk about it and write your ideas.
3. **(a)** Write a list of games from the past that are still played today. **(b)** Write a list of pastimes and games that are not played anymore. **(c)** Write a list of new games from recent times.
4. Why do you think some games live on, while others disappear?

D. Get Creative.

1. Read a section or chapter from each of the novels, *Jimeen* by P. Ó Siochfhradha and *Just William* by Richmal Crompton. How would you describe the characters? Do you like them?
2. Pair work: Interview some adults such as your parents, grandparents or teachers. Ask them about the games they played when they were children. Find out if the games were played outdoors or indoors, how they were played and which ones were their favourites. Report back to the class.

E. Digging Deeper

1. Use the internet to find out the rhymes that were used in street games in the past. Record them on a CD and make an illustrated class book.
2. The cups presented to the All-Ireland Hurling and Football Championship winners are named after two people. Find out who those people were and what they did for Irish sport.

Strand: Local Studies **Strand Unit:** Games and Pastimes in the Past

Unit 7: The Bronze Age

New Words
fulacht fiadh · wattle and daub · smelting · artefact · barter · currach · trackway
standing stones · stone circles

Timeline

World | **Ireland**

- 2500 BC — Stonehenge is built in England
- 2400 BC — Europe's earliest copper mining begins at Ross Island, Kerry
- 2000 BC — Wheeled carts are used in Eastern Europe
- 1800 BC — England and Scandinavia begin trading tin and precious stones
- 1500 BC
- 1200 AD — Goldsmiths making jewellery
- Bronze trumpets are made
- 1000 BC
- 776 BC First Olympic Games held at Olympia in Greece
- 753 BC City of Rome is founded
- 600 BC Wooden block wheels are used on carts
- 500 BC

Life during the Bronze Age

The Bronze Age lasted for nearly 2000 years, from about 2600 BC to 600 BC. Life was not easy for most people during that time. They had to work very hard at clearing forests, farming, building and mining. During the Bronze Age, the weather became very wet and there were long cold spells. During times of bad weather, some areas of farmland were flooded and the crops were ruined. Farmers had to try to produce more food on the areas of good land. Thieves often came to steal food and the farmers' tools.

Homes

Bronze Age houses were circular. They were 5 m to 7 m wide and they had only one room. The builders began building the house by driving strong wooden posts into the ground. They wove light branches from trees between the posts to make a 'wattle' wall. Next, they made a type of plaster called 'daub' from mud and straw and they used this to cover the walls. They used straw or reeds to make a thatched roof. Often they made other similar buildings to house animals. They surrounded the buildings with a stone wall, wooden fence or bank of earth, depending on the kind of materials they found in the area. The wall protected the people from wild animals, enemies and thieves.

Bronze Age homes

Children building a wattle wall

Strand: Early People and Ancient Societies   Strand Unit: Bronze Age Peoples

Farming

Archaeologists have examined the bones and teeth of animals found in Bronze Age middens. They also examined seeds and pollen to find out what kind of plants or crops were grown at that time. They discovered that Bronze Age people kept cattle, sheep, goats and pigs. They grew crops of wheat and barley, which they used to make porridge and bread. They also grew flax, which they used for making cloth. Flax fibres are even stronger than cotton fibres and the flax seeds gave them oil for lighting. Growing crops and keeping animals is called 'mixed farming'.

Flax

Hot History

For cooking, Bronze Age people made a wood or stone pit called a 'fulacht fiadh'. They poured water into the pit and boiled it by adding red-hot stones. Meat was wrapped in straw and cooked in the boiling water. The straw allowed the meat to float, making it easier to lift out.

Fulacht fiadh

Mining for copper

One of the most important things to happen in the Bronze Age was that the people began using metal to make stronger, harder tools and weapons. At first they used copper, which is found in rocks in Ireland. Bronze Age miners worked out a way of getting the copper out of the rocks by setting the rocks on fire! When the rocks were red-hot, they threw cold water on them, causing them to crack. They used stone hammers to break the rocks into smaller pieces, which they heated again. As the copper heated up, it melted and flowed out of the rocks. This way of getting metal from rocks is known as smelting. The copper was then given to smiths to make tools, weapons and ornaments.

Stone hammer and copper

Bronze and gold

Later, the metalworkers discovered that by adding tin to the copper, they could make a much harder and more useful metal. The new metal was bronze. Tin was brought over from Cornwall in England. Gold was also used during this time in Ireland. Bronze and gold were used to make beautiful objects, or artefacts.

Bronze cup found in the River Shannon

Strand: Early People and Ancient Societies Strand Unit: Bronze Age Peoples

Bronze Age artefacts found in Ireland:

Tools	Weapons	Jewellery	Musical Instruments
knives axes needles razors cauldrons	swords spears shields daggers	collars rings bracelets dress fasteners earrings armlets	trumpets horns rattles bells

Hot History

Bronze Age people wore lots of heavy clothes to stay warm. However, there were no zips or Velcro to keep the clothes closed. Someone invented a pin to fasten the clothes in place. How clever!

Bronze pin

Gold collars

Gold shield

Bronze axes

ACTIVITIES

1. Match the words in column A with the explanations in column B.

A	B
archaeologist	• a crop grown for making cloth and giving oil
blacksmith	• a water-filled pit used for cooking
fulacht fiadh	• a person who studies ancient remains
flax	• a person who makes metal objects
smelting	• old/ancient objects
artefacts	• a method of separating a metal from rock

2. Pair work: *Bronze Age people were great at solving problems.* Do you agree or disagree with this statement? Talk about it with your partner and then write your answer.
3. List the steps for getting copper from rock in Bronze Age times.

Strand: Early People and Ancient Societies   Strand Unit: Bronze Age Peoples

TRADE AND TRAVEL

As time went on, Bronze Age metalworkers could not always find the things they needed in the places where they lived. They began travelling to trade their goods for the materials and objects that they wanted. However, they did not use money for buying and selling. Instead, they swapped things to get what they needed. Swapping goods as payment is known as barter.

TRANSPORT

We know that horses and oxen were used from the beginning of the Bronze Age. However, archaeologists are not sure if the Bronze Age people actually rode the horses or if they just used them for pulling carts. Travel by boat was important, as there are lots of rivers and lakes in Ireland. Two kinds of boats were used during the Bronze Age. One was a boat that looked like a canoe, made from a tree trunk that had been split lengthwise in half. The wood on the inside of the trunk was dug out using an axe. The other was a boat that was covered in leather. This type of boat was quite common. It looked like the currach that is still in use in the West of Ireland.

Modern dugout canoe

Hot History

Bronze Age metalworkers discovered that when copper is left in the open air, it changes colour from copper to green/blue. Evidence of this change can be seen in Dublin on the roof of the Four Courts.

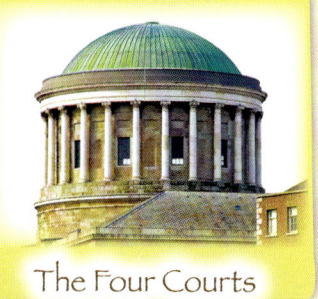

The Four Courts

Currach

TRACKWAYS THROUGH WETLANDS

Large parts of Ireland were covered with bog and marsh and Bronze Age people had to think of ways to get across them with their animals and carts. They were good at inventing, so they came up with the idea of building paths, or trackways, through the wetlands. First, they laid thick branches on top of the boggy ground. Then they placed wooden planks on top of the branches. It was easy to travel across the wooden planks. The Bronze Age people also had another method of building trackways by weaving hazel sticks together to make 'hurdles'. The hurdles were laid on top of the bog. You could say that the Bronze Age trackways were our first roads.

Hurdles

Strand: Early People and Ancient Societies Strand Unit: Bronze Age Peoples

Religion and ceremonies

As we know, people in Stone Age times built tombs and monuments to honour their dead. Religious ceremonies were very important to Bronze Age people, too. They probably believed that life went on after death and they treated their dead with great respect. Sometimes the body of a dead person was burned and the ashes were placed in a vase, or urn. At other times, the body was placed in a grave or tomb, along with some objects like pottery bowls, daggers and beads. Poulnabrone Dolmen in the Burren, County Clare, is a tomb.

Poulnabrone Dolmen

Standing stones

Bronze Age monuments can still be seen around Ireland. Standing stones are one example. Standing stones were probably used to mark the area where ancient meetings took place or where an important person was buried.

Standing stone, Valencia Island, County Kerry

Hot History
The largest standing stone in Ireland is in Tamnarry, County Kildare. It is 7 m high. It fell down in 1931, but it was put back up again three years later.

Hot History
It seems that living in the Bronze Age was not very good for your health. Most people died before the age of 40 years.

Stone circles

Near the end of the Bronze Age, another type of monument became popular. Bronze Age people built stone circles in Ulster and Munster. It is thought that the stone circles may have been used by astronomers to mark special events during the year. Lots of people probably came to celebrate those events. The events would have been times to talk and share stories. Trumpets, drums, bells and rattles could have been used to make music. However, by 600 BC, the Bronze Age was coming to an end. A new, wonderful discovery had been made and the Iron Age was about to begin!

Drombeg Stone Circle, County Cork

Strand: Early People and Ancient Societies   Strand Unit: Bronze Age Peoples

ACTIVITIES

A. Can You Remember?

1. What two metals were mixed together to make bronze?
2. What was the weather like in Bronze Age Ireland?
3. About what time did the Bronze Age begin?
4. What was the shape and size of a Bronze Age house?
5. What is flax and what was it used for?

B. Choose the Correct Answer to Complete Each Sentence.

1. The Bronze Age lasted for nearly _____ years.
   A. 200, **B.** 2000, **C.** 20,000, **or D.** 20
2. Hurdles were made from _____.
   A. animal skins, **B.** hazel sticks, **C.** planks, or **D.** spears
3. Smelting was done to _____.
   A. cook food, **B.** grow crops, **C.** get copper from rock, or **D.** heat wood
4. Bronze Age people used barter to _____.
   A. clear forests, **B.** make trackways, **C.** swap goods, or **D.** cook food

C. Think About It.

1. Imagine that you are a Bronze Age farmer using bronze tools. Your neighbour is still using stone tools. Explain to him or her why your tools are better.
2. Look back to Unit 2. What are the differences between the Stone Age way of cooking meat and the 'fulacht fiadh' method that the Bronze Age people used?
3. Why do you think objects like weapons and jewellery were buried with the dead?
4. Why do you think objects like axes and jewellery have survived from the Bronze Age, but clothes have not survived?

D. Get Creative.

1. Plan a menu for a special event in your Bronze Age family. Write the food you will choose, the way you will get it and the way you will cook it.
2. (a) Describe some of the problems that were faced by the Bronze Age people.
   (b) Describe the ways in which we deal with similar problems today.
3. Choose objects in your classroom that would help archaeologists 1000 years from now to build up a picture of what life was like for you. Only some objects will last that long. Why will some objects last that long while others will not?

E. Digging Deeper

The use of metal made a big difference to the lives of Bronze Age people. Talk to your grandparents and parents. Make a list of the 10 most important developments that have occurred during their lives.

Strand: Early People and Ancient Societies   Strand Unit: Bronze Age Peoples

Unit 8: Saint Brendan

New Words

navigator · cells · Hy-brasil · explorer · manuscript · monastery

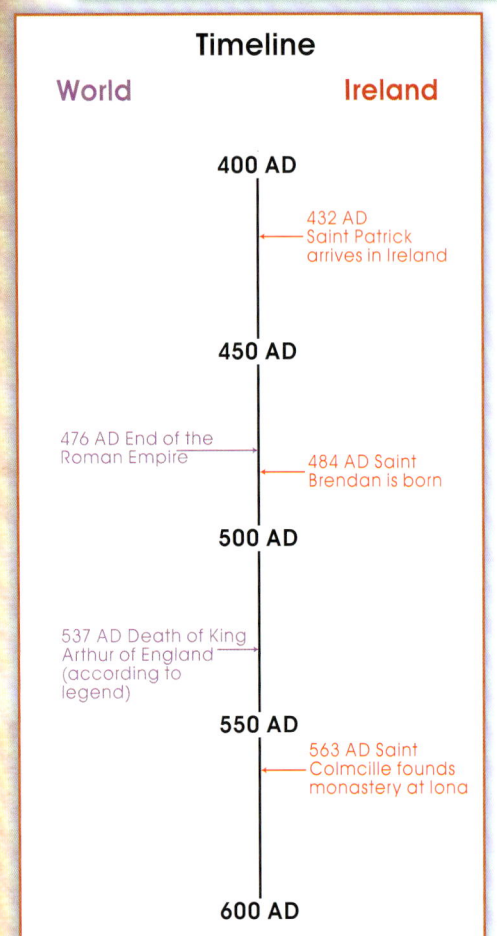

Timeline

World	Ireland
400 AD	
	432 AD Saint Patrick arrives in Ireland
450 AD	
476 AD End of the Roman Empire	484 AD Saint Brendan is born
500 AD	
537 AD Death of King Arthur of England (according to legend)	
550 AD	563 AD Saint Colmcille founds monastery at Iona
600 AD	

BRENDAN AS A YOUNG BOY

Saint Brendan was born near Tralee in County Kerry in 484 AD. He is one of the most famous Irish saints and he is known as 'Brendan the Navigator'. For the first five years of his life, Brendan was taught by a nun called Sister Ita of Munster. As a young boy, Brendan spent many hours staring out to sea and wondering what was beyond the horizon of the Atlantic Ocean.

BRENDAN THE PRIEST

When Brendan grew up, he decided that he wanted to become a priest. Bishop Erc of Galway ordained Brendan as a priest in 512 AD. Between 512 and 530 AD, Brendan built small huts, or cells, at Ardfert and Shanakeel. Both of those places are at the foot of Mount Brandon in County Kerry. Cells were small beehive-shaped huts, in which monks prayed. However, Brendan still dreamed of being an explorer. He longed to discover the lost island of Hy-Brasil. According to legend, Hy-Brasil was a beautiful island to the west of Ireland. Brendan wanted to prove that it was a real place. Brendan finally set sail from a place near Mount Brandon, on a voyage towards the island.

Ardfert Cathedral

42   **Strand:** Story   **Strand Unit:** Myths and Legends

The Brendan Voyage

Brendan is said to have sailed with a group of 16 monks to the island of Hy-Brasil. They sailed for seven years and they had many adventures along the way. They were guided by the stars at night and by the sun during the day. They took turns keeping watch at night-time. Their most famous adventure happened when, after many days sailing, they reached a smooth, black island. The monks were delighted to see land and they jumped out of the boat. They lit a fire and began to prepare breakfast. Suddenly the island moved! All of the monks were thrown into the water. The 'island' was actually a sleeping whale, which was awoken by the monks cooking breakfast on its back!

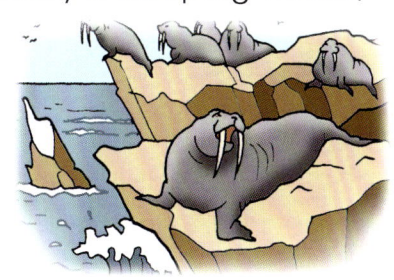

A harsh land

The monks sailed on and they came to an ocean covered with fog. They passed a huge floating mountain that was the colour of silver. It was actually an iceberg, but it was the first one that the crew had ever seen. Next they sighted land, but it was a harsh place with jagged cliffs, where great beasts roared loudly. The animals had cat-like heads and bronze-coloured eyes. Those loud creatures were actually walruses and the land was Greenland.

Paradise!

They sailed south and, finally, they sighted land again. This time, the land was green and sunny. It was a beautiful place, filled with wonderful flowers and very colourful birds. This could have been the Bahamas, or even Florida in America. It seemed like a paradise to Brendan and his weary crew. Many people believe that Saint Brendan was the first European to arrive in America, long before Christopher Columbus landed there.

Hot History

Hy-Brasil was not a real place, but it is mentioned in many Irish legends. It was believed to be covered in mist, which cleared for one day every seven years. On that day, it could be seen, but no one could reach it.

Hot History

In 2011, the Central Bank of Ireland produced special €10 coins celebrating Saint Brendan the Navigator. The coin shows Brendan sailing towards America.

Strand: Story Strand Unit: Myths and Legends 43

RETURN TO IRELAND

When Brendan returned to Ireland, the story of his amazing journey spread far and wide. Many people came to Ardfert. Brendan built more cells at Gallarus, County Kerry, and at Brandon Hill, County Kilkenny. He then travelled to Scotland and Wales, but he returned to Ireland after three years. He built a monastery in Clonfert, County Galway, in 570 AD. Clonfert was one of Ireland's most important monasteries. At one point, it had 3000 monks. Brendan died in Clonfert in 577 AD and his feast day is celebrated on May 16th. He is the patron saint of sailors and navigators.

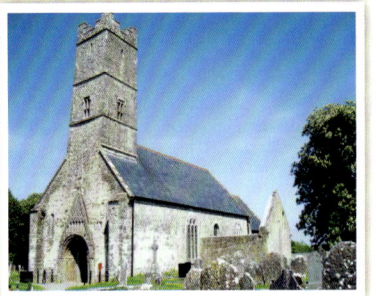

Prayer room at Gallarus

Clonfert Cathedral

BRENDAN'S KNOWLEDGE

The story of Brendan's voyage was popular in Europe during the Middle Ages. Christopher Columbus is said to have heard the story before he sailed to America. The manuscript, *Voyage of Saint Brendan*, talks about Brendan's knowledge of foreign plants and animals. He could only have gained this knowledge by visiting faraway lands.

Hot History

In the ninth century, a handwritten book, or manuscript, was written about Brendan. The manuscript was called *Navigatio Sancti Brendani*, or *Voyage of Saint Brendan*.

TIM SEVERIN

On May 17th, 1976, an explorer called Tim Severin took the same route that Brendan had taken. Tim and his five-man crew left Kerry in a boat that was a copy, or replica, of the one that Brendan had sailed in. It was covered with 49 ox hides, stitched together and stretched over a wooden frame. He wanted to prove that the journey Brendan had made was possible. He also wanted to show that Brendan could have arrived in America before Columbus. His boat was named *Brendan*. It took over a year to complete the journey. His boat got damaged near Iceland and he was delayed there until the boat was repaired. Then he sailed past Greenland and finally reached Newfoundland in Canada. In 1978, he wrote a book called *The Brendan Voyage*. He proved that it was possible for a leather-covered boat like Saint Brendan's to reach America.

Tim Severin in the boat, Brendan

Strand: Story **Strand Unit:** Myths and Legends

ACTIVITIES

A. Can You Remember?

1. What was the floating mountain that Brendan and his crew saw?
2. What were the strange beasts with cat-like heads that they saw?
3. Brendan built his first cells near which Irish mountain?
4. What was the name of Tim Severin's boat?
5. How was Saint Brendan celebrated in 2011?

B. Choose the Correct Answer to Complete Each Sentence.

1. Brendan was born near _____ .
   A. Ardfert, B. Dingle, C. Tralee, or D. Shanakeel
2. Brendan had always longed to be an _____ .
   A. astronaut, B. explorer, C. inventor, or D. author
3. Clonfert was an important Irish _____ .
   A. monastery, B. university, C. cell, or D. island
4. Brendan's voyage was known to _____ .
   A. King Arthur, B. Saint Patrick, C. Saint Colmcille, or D. Columbus

C. Think About It.

1. Why do you think the sailors were on watch at night?
2. Write two reasons why manuscripts are important.
3. Describe the route that Brendan took on his voyage, by writing the places where he landed in the correct order.

D. Get Creative.

1. Act out the scene that would have taken place on the whale's back.
2. Pair work: Discuss and then write about how Brendan and his crew must have felt when they thought they had reached the island of Hy-brasil.
3. Design a logo or a picture to put on the sail of Brendan's boat.
4. Do you think that Brendan's life was interesting? Write two reasons for your answer.

E. Digging Deeper

1. Listen to the music, 'The Brendan Voyage' by Shaun Davey. Try to identify the places, birds, animals and adventures.
2. Use the internet to find out about the Saint Brendan monument in County Kerry.
3. Use the internet to find out about the Brendan Boat Craggaunowen Project. Your teacher will give you a list of words to key into a search engine.
4. Read *Saint Brendan and the Voyage Before Columbus* by Michael Mc Grew (Paulist Press).

Strand: Story   Strand Unit: Myths and Legends

Unit 9: The Egyptians

New Words

nomad   Pharaoh   pyramid   papyrus   silt   mummified   hieroglyphs   Senet

Timeline

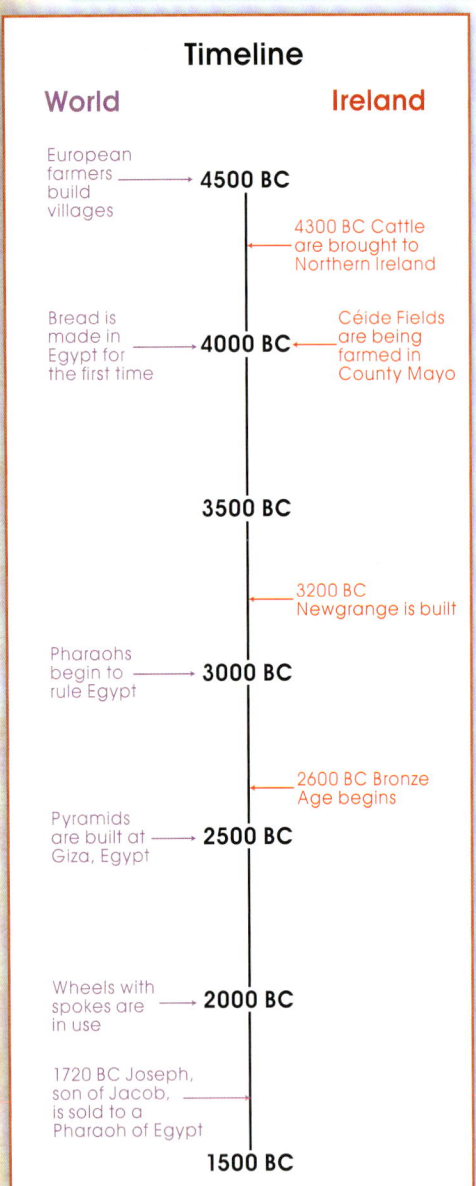

World		Ireland
European farmers build villages	4500 BC	
		4300 BC Cattle are brought to Northern Ireland
Bread is made in Egypt for the first time	4000 BC	Céide Fields are being farmed in County Mayo
	3500 BC	
		3200 BC Newgrange is built
Pharaohs begin to rule Egypt	3000 BC	
		2600 BC Bronze Age begins
Pyramids are built at Giza, Egypt	2500 BC	
Wheels with spokes are in use	2000 BC	
1720 BC Joseph, son of Jacob, is sold to a Pharaoh of Egypt		
	1500 BC	

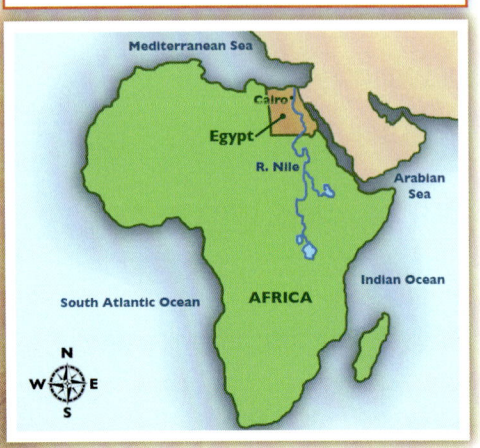

Ancient Egypt

The first Egyptians were nomads. Nomads travel from place to place in search of food and water. Around the year 3000 BC, the Egyptians began to settle in the areas of rich soil along the banks of the River Nile. Over time, the Pharaohs (Egyptian kings), made a huge empire by defeating the nearby tribes and taking their lands. They made slaves of the people from the defeated tribes. The Pharaohs ruled from around 3000 BC until the birth of Christ. The Egyptians believed that the Pharaoh was a god who had come down to earth from the skies. They adored him and feared him, because he had the power to let them live or die. The Pharaohs had great wealth, which they used to build pyramids, temples and statues to honour themselves and their gods.

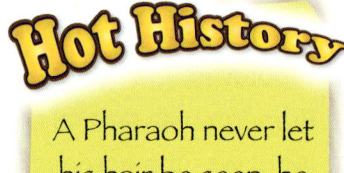

The River Nile

Egypt is covered by a desert, so most of the country is not suited to farming and growing crops. However, the River Nile flows through the desert and people have been living alongside it since ancient times. The Egyptians believed that the world was flat and circular and that the Nile flowed through its centre!

Hot History

A Pharaoh never let his hair be seen; he always wore a headdress called a Nemes.

Hot History

Pyramids were the tombs of the Pharaohs. It took many thousands of workers to build them.

Pyramid at Giza

Strand: Early People and Ancient Societies   **Strand Unit:** Egyptians

Farming along the Nile

Every year, the Nile flooded the land along its banks. The floods left plenty of water on the land. The floods also left behind a rich mud called silt, which made the soil very fertile (good for farming). Crops grew well in the moist, fertile soil and they produced large amounts of food. The Egyptians grew crops of wheat, from which they made bread. Bread was their most important food. They also grew green beans, onions, lettuce and leeks. As there was plenty of food, the number of people living along the banks of the river grew. The Nile helped the people in other ways. Boats were made from reeds, which grew in the shallow waters of the Nile. People were able to travel from place to place by boat. Larger wooden boats were used to carry heavy goods. Reeds were also used to make a type of paper known as papyrus. The Egyptians also hunted waterfowl such as ducks and geese, which lived along the banks of the river.

Towns, homes and gardens

Many workers were needed to build the pyramids. Towns and cities grew along the banks of the Nile, at the sites where the pyramids were being built. Thick walls were built around the towns and dirt roads were laid out in a grid. The roads had a stone channel, or drain, running down the centre. Important officials lived in one part of the town and the craft workers and poor people lived in another part of the town. Temples were made from stone. Other buildings were built with mud bricks. Most Egyptian houses had roofs that were held up by logs from palm trees. The floors of the houses were made of packed earth. The homes of wealthy Egyptians often had walls that were plastered and painted. They also had bedrooms, living rooms, a kitchen, workshops and a courtyard. The furniture included beds, chairs, stools and benches. In the cool evenings, families would sit on their flat roofs or else walk and talk in their gardens.

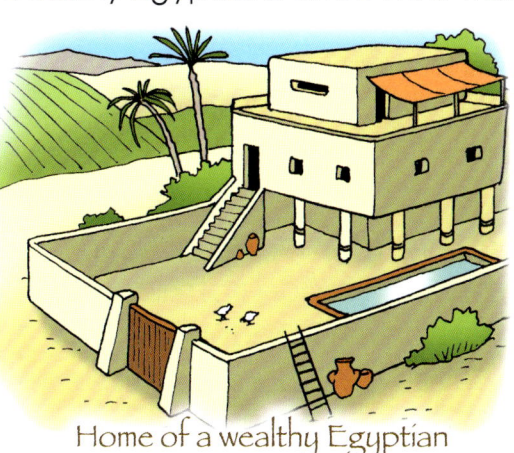

Home of a wealthy Egyptian

Hot History

The streets of New York are also laid out in a grid. A grid is useful for working out an exact location.

New York

Hot History

Egyptian bricks were made from soft clay mixed with straw. They were left to dry in the heat of the sun.

FOOD AND BANQUETS

Instead of being paid with money, workers were paid with food. They ate bread, onions and salted fish and they drank beer. Bakers made all sorts of cakes and loaves. We know that the flour contained hard bits, because the teeth of mummies show a lot of wear and tear. A banquet was a great event, where rich people ate roasted goose, stewed beef, duck, gazelle (a type of antelope), cheese, and vegetables stewed in milk. Wine was served from stone jars that were labelled with the name of the vineyard and the year the wine was produced.

CLOTHES

Most Egyptians' clothes were made from linen. They used a loom to weave fibres from flax plants into linen thread. The climate was very hot, so people wore very little clothing. Men tied a piece of cloth around their waists like a kilt. Women wore simple dresses. Egyptian children wore nothing until they became teenagers. Wealthy people enjoyed dressing up in stylish clothes and jewellery made from fine materials. Men and women wore green eyeshadow, black eyeliner, red lipstick and perfume. The Egyptians also liked to tattoo their skin. Rich people wore wigs, while poorer people wore their hair long or in pigtails. Until boys were 12 years old, their heads were shaved to protect them from lice and fleas. They kept just one plaited piece of hair.

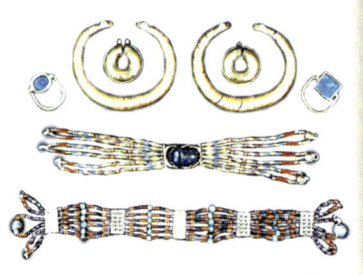

Ancient Egyptian jewellery

Hot History

When a Pharaoh died, his body was preserved, or mummified. The organs were removed and the body was treated with a chemical and wrapped in linen bandages. Cats were special animals, so they were also mummified!

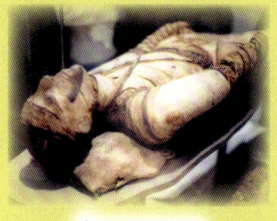

A mummy

CHILDREN'S LIVES

The sons of rich people went to school, where they learned to read and write. Pictures known as hieroglyphs were used instead of letters and words. A sentence was made by drawing a number of hieroglyphs in a column. Children wrote on papyrus using pens made from reeds. The ink was made from soot, red soil and glue. In their free time, children played with wooden animals, spinning tops and dolls. Sometimes they played a board game called Senet. They also enjoyed swimming, music, dancing and keeping pets.

Hieroglyphic letters on papyrus

Senet

Strand: Early People and Ancient Societies **Strand Unit:** Egyptians

ACTIVITIES

A. Can You Remember?

1. Who were the rulers of Ancient Egypt?
2. Name three crops that were grown by the Egyptians.
3. How did the soil along the banks of the River Nile become fertile?
4. What foods were eaten at an Egyptian banquet?
5. Describe the ways in which the rich Egyptians liked to dress.

B. Choose the Correct Answer to Complete Each Sentence.

1. Papyrus was a type of _____.
   A. paper, B. book, C. pen, or D. ink
2. The pyramids were the _____ of the Pharaohs.
   A. houses, B. tombs, C. workshops, or D. schools
3. Hieroglyphs were Egyptian _____.
   A. paintings, B. letters, C. tattoos, or D. pens
4. Senet was a type of _____.
   A. game, B. food, C. pen, or D. boat

C. Think About It.

1. Why do you think the Egyptians adored and feared the Pharaohs?
2. Write two reasons why so many people lived on the banks of the Nile.
3. What would you have liked about living in Ancient Egypt? What would you have disliked?
4. Why do you think the Egyptians mummified bodies?
5. Do you think that using hieroglyphs was a good way of writing?

D. Get Creative.

1. Act out a scene from an Egyptian banquet, with the Pharaoh as the guest of honour.
2. You are a worker on the building site of a new pyramid. Write a letter home to your family, who live on the bank of the River Nile.
3. Imagine that you are a schoolboy in Ancient Egypt. Write a report for your diary.
4. Write a sentence in hieroglyphs, using paint and a thin paintbrush.

E. Digging Deeper

1. Listen to the music, *Aida* by Verdi, which is an opera about Ancient Egypt.
2. Use the internet to find out about Egyptian myths or legends. Rewrite one in your own words or write your own legend.
3. Compare the people from the Bronze Age to the Ancient Egyptians. In what ways were they different? In what ways were they the same?

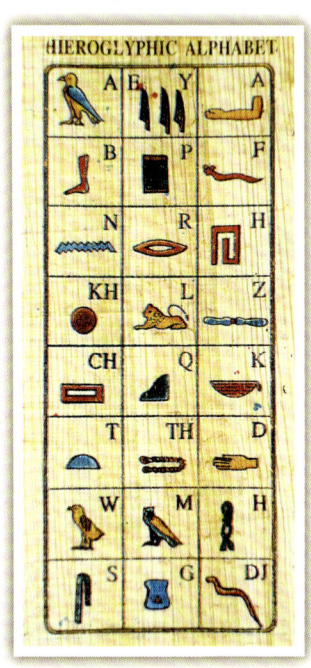

Strand: Early People and Ancient Societies Strand Unit: Egyptians

Unit 10: The Wooden Horse of Troy

New Words

Sparta   Troy   Athens

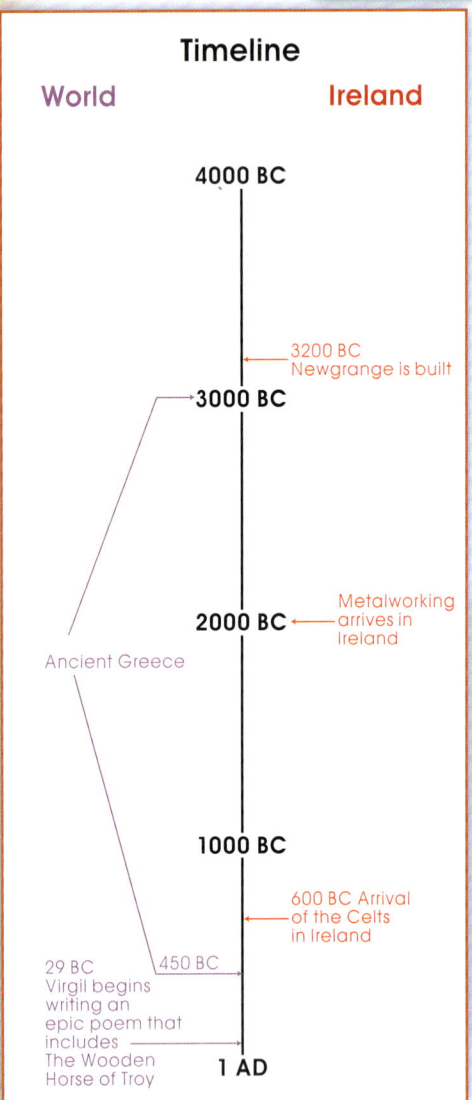

Timeline

World | Ireland

- 4000 BC
- 3200 BC Newgrange is built
- 3000 BC
- Metalworking arrives in Ireland
- 2000 BC
- Ancient Greece
- 1000 BC
- 600 BC Arrival of the Celts in Ireland
- 450 BC
- 29 BC Virgil begins writing an epic poem that includes The Wooden Horse of Troy
- 1 AD

KING MENELAUS

Long, long ago in Ancient Greece, King Menelaus ruled over a city called Sparta. Sparta and Athens were two of the most powerful cities in Ancient Greece. King Menelaus was married to a beautiful woman called Helen. Menelaus and Helen decided to invite Paris, the son of the King of Troy, to visit them. While Paris was staying with them, he and Helen fell in love. One night, when everyone was asleep, Paris and Helen ran away from Sparta and they sailed to Troy. When Menelaus found out what they had done, he was very upset and angry.

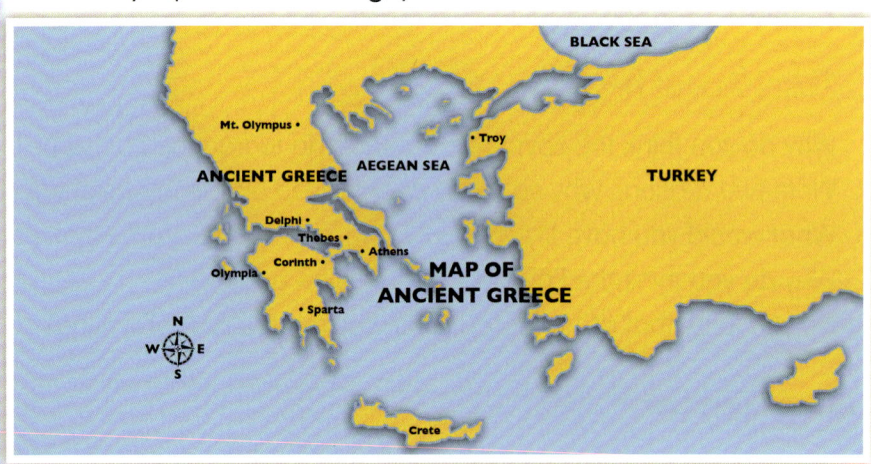

MAP OF ANCIENT GREECE

Menelaus

JOURNEY TO TROY

Menelaus decided to follow them and bring Helen back to Greece. Over the next two years, he gathered a huge army. When everything was ready, they set sail for Troy (in what is now called Turkey). Many other Greek kings and their armies sailed with Menelaus. When they arrived in Troy, they found that the city was protected by tall, strong walls. The Greeks tried to break down the walls and the gates, but they were driven back by the Trojans.

A LONG WAR

For 10 years, the Greeks surrounded the city of Troy. During that time, there were many battles. The Greeks' greatest warrior was called Achilles. The Trojans' greatest warrior was Hector, the brother of Paris. Achilles and Hector fought each other many times, until Achilles finally killed Hector. Achilles tied Hector's body to his chariot and he dragged it along the ground beside the gates of Troy. The Trojans were very upset when they saw this happening to their hero. Paris was especially angry. He knew that Achilles had one weak spot and he knew exactly where it was. He took a poisoned arrow and aimed it at Achilles' heel. The arrow went straight into Achilles' heel and killed him.

Attacking the city of Troy

ODYSSEUS' PLAN

After 10 years of war, the Greeks finally gave up hope of capturing Troy and of getting Helen back. Their leaders held a meeting. "We should return home to Greece," said one king. "Too many of our soldiers are being killed," said another. Menelaus did not want to leave without Helen. A king called Odysseus spoke up. "I have a plan to trick the Trojans," he said. They all listened carefully as Odysseus explained his plan. "Let's pretend to sail away," he said. "We'll leave a gift for the Trojans – a gift to tell them that we want to end the war. The gift will be a wooden horse. The horse is the symbol of Troy, so they'll love it. This horse will be very special, as it will have 30 of our best warriors hidden inside. The Trojans will see the horse and bring it inside the gates. Our men will wait until dark and then sneak out and open the gates, so that we can attack!"

In those days, if an army decided to end a war, they usually gave their enemy a gift. It could be a gift of slaves, a statue or money. The Greeks agreed that Odysseus' plan was good.

The kings hold a meeting

Hot History

Soon after he was born, Achilles' mother dipped him in the River Styx, because it had magical powers that would protect him from harm. However, because she held him by his heel, it did not touch the water. Today, if someone has a weak spot, we call it their 'Achilles' heel'.

Strand: Story Strand Unit: Myths and Legends 51

Building the horse

That night, the Greeks gathered lots of wood and built a huge wooden horse. It had a secret door, which led to a hollow space inside. A group of 30 warriors climbed inside to hide, closing the door behind them. The Greeks pulled the horse towards Troy and left it outside the gates. The Greeks took down their tents, went back to their ships and sailed away from Troy. The Trojans were overjoyed because they thought they had won. They hoped they would never see the Greeks again.

The wooden horse

Celebrations

The Greeks sailed behind a nearby island and hid their ships. The Trojans opened the gates and went out to see the horse. "What will we do with this?" asked one man. "Bring it into the city," said another. An old woman said, "Burn it here on the shore. It will only bring us bad luck." Just then a group of Trojan warriors came along with a captured Greek soldier. "Why did the Greeks build this horse and leave it here?" demanded a Trojan leader. The Greek soldier explained that the horse was a special gift, which would protect Troy if it was placed inside the city. The Trojans pulled the horse inside the gates, thinking that the city would be safe at last. They held a great party, which went on late into the night. When the party was over, the Trojans went to bed, tired but happy.

Captured Greek soldier

Capturing Troy

Greeks attacking Troy

Hot History

The saying, 'Beware of Greeks bearing gifts', comes from the story of the Wooden Horse of Troy!

As soon as the city was quiet, the Greek warriors climbed out of the horse and opened the city gates. By now, the Greek ships had sailed back to Troy and they were waiting at the shore. They entered the city, killing people and burning the buildings. Many Trojans died that night, including Paris. The great city of Troy was captured and burned to the ground. The Greeks then sailed back home. Helen returned home to Sparta with her husband, Menelaus. The Greeks had won a famous victory, but many of them were sad about all of the people who had died on both sides. Some wondered if the battle of Troy should ever have been fought.

ACTIVITIES

A. Can You Remember?

1. What was the name of Helen's husband?
2. Who was the greatest Greek warrior?
3. For how many years did the Greeks fight the Trojans?
4. What did the Greeks leave outside the city gates?
5. How was the city of Troy finally captured?

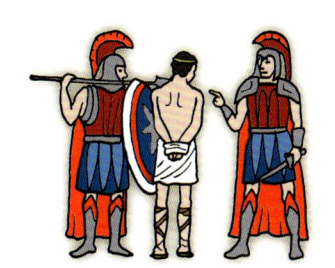

B. Choose the Correct Answer to Complete Each Sentence.

1. Menelaus wanted to bring Helen back to _____.
   A. Troy, B. Sparta, C. Athens, or D. the River Styx
2. The city of Troy was protected by _____.
   A. a river, B. barbed wire, C. strong walls, or D. deep trenches
3. Odysseus came up with _____ to defeat the Trojans.
   A. weapons, B. more ships, C. a plan, or D. a dream
4. The city of Sparta was in _____.
   A. Troy, B. Greece, C. Athens, or D. Turkey

C. Think About It.

1. Do you think that fighting a war was the best way for Menelaus to solve the problem of Helen and Paris? Could he have found another way?
2. Why do you think the other Greek kings sailed with Menelaus to bring Helen back?
3. Why do you think Achilles dragged Hector's body behind his chariot?
4. Do you think the Trojans were foolish to have been tricked by the Greeks?

D. Get Creative.

1. Do you think that Helen wanted to go back to Sparta? Write a letter from Helen to her best friend, decribing how she feels.
2. Pair work: Write a Greek newspaper report on how Troy was captured. Your partner should write a *Trojan* newspaper report on how Troy was captured.
3. Write the conversation between Paris and Helen, when they saw the Greeks sailing away.
4. You are a Greek king. Think of a different plan for getting into the city of Troy.

E. Digging Deeper

1. Read the book, *Return to Troy* by Pierce C. Feirtear (Blackwater Press).
2. Use the internet to find out more about Troy and see a video of the Wooden Horse. Your teacher will give you a list of words to key into a search engine.

Strand: Story   Strand Unit: Myths and Legends

Unit 11: Schools and Education

New Words

lyre　ludi　slate　scroll　stylus　abacus　fostering　hedge schools　gallery　copperplate

Timeline

World | Ireland

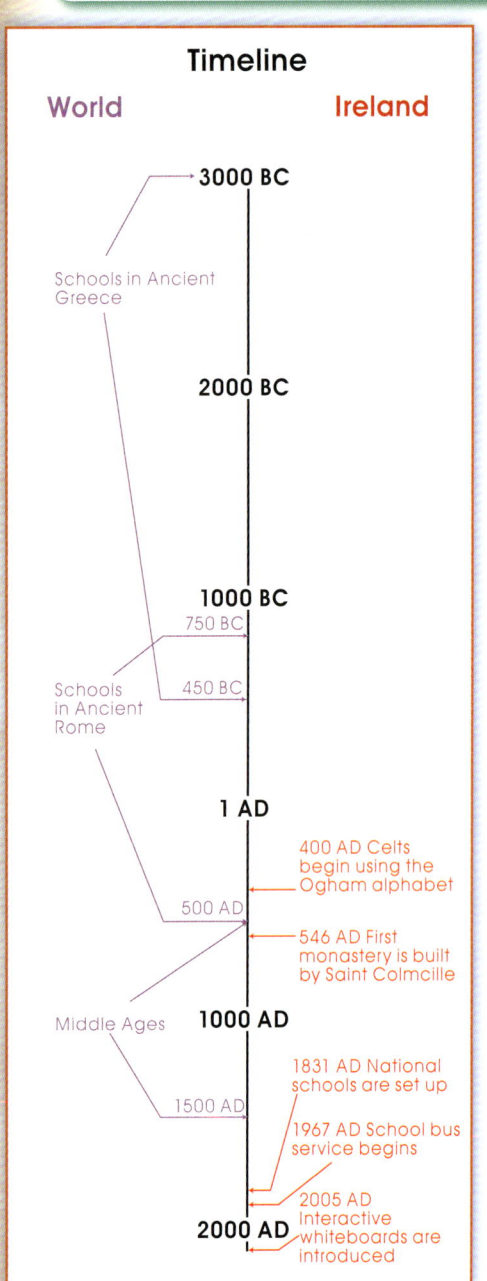

- 3000 BC
- Schools in Ancient Greece
- 2000 BC
- 1000 BC
- 750 BC
- Schools in Ancient Rome
- 450 BC
- 1 AD
- 400 AD Celts begin using the Ogham alphabet
- 500 AD
- 546 AD First monastery is built by Saint Colmcille
- 1000 AD
- Middle Ages
- 1831 AD National schools are set up
- 1500 AD
- 1967 AD School bus service begins
- 2005 AD Interactive whiteboards are introduced
- 2000 AD

Education in Ancient Greece

Before the first schools were built, children learned from their parents. If parents were able to read and write, they taught their children, too. Children also learned how to help on the farm and in the home.

In Ancient Greece, only boys went to school. Girls learned to read and write at home. Boys attended primary school between the ages of six and 14. Afterwards, they could attend high school until they were 18 years old. Parents in Ancient Greece had to pay for their children's education, so the children of poor people could not go to school.

Schools in Ancient Greece

Boys in Ancient Greece went to school to study Maths, Art and Drama. They also learned how the government worked. A big difference between now and then was *how* children learned. Books were scarce, so children had to learn things by heart. Stories such as the Wooden Horse of Troy were told in poems that were learned by heart. Teachers made it easier by getting the children to sing the poems! Sometimes the teacher played along on an instrument called a lyre, which sounded a bit like a guitar. All of the teachers were men. Physical training was important, as boys would have to protect Greece from attackers when they grew up. Men went to military school (school for soldiers) for two years between the ages of 18 and 20.

Ancient Greek school

Lyre

54　Strand: Continuity and Change Over Time　Strand Unit: Schools and Education

Schools in Ancient Rome

In Ancient Rome, schools were called 'ludi' (the word for 'play' in Latin is 'ludus'). Children started school when they were six years old. Boys and girls went to separate schools, where they learned to read scrolls and books. They used a stylus to write on tablets made of wooden boards covered with wax. A stylus had a pointed end and a flat end. It was usually made of bronze or iron. Children scratched letters into the wax tablet with the pointed end. The flat end was used for rubbing out. School began before sunrise, so children brought candles to school and used them until daybreak. Learning to speak well in public was very important. Like the Ancient Greeks, the Romans also did a lot of physical training.

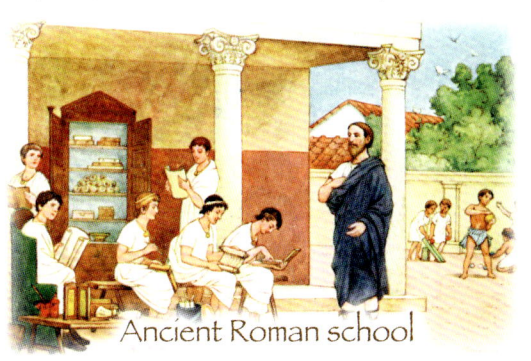

Ancient Roman school

Hot History
A scroll was a roll of papyrus, which was used like a page.

Ancient Roman tablet and stylus

Roman numerals

Children in Ancient Rome did not learn a lot of Mathematics. They used pebbles and a counting frame, or abacus, to help them when they did sums. Roman numerals were used for counting. Roman numerals are sometimes used today, but the trouble is, they take up a lot of space! For example, 78 is written as LXXVIII and 6000 is written as MMMMMM.

The Middle Ages

During the Middle Ages, poor children were only educated at home or in the fields. The sons of wealthy lords and landowners were often sent away to the castles of lords to train as knights. From the age of seven or eight, they learned archery, sword fighting, riding, reading, writing, chess and any other skills that they would need as a knight. Boys from less wealthy families sometimes learned a craft like stone carving, carpentry or candle making. They also left home at eight years old and went to live with a master craftsman. Girls sometimes trained in a craft like embroidery or dressmaking.

Dressmaking

Strand: Continuity and Change Over Time   Strand Unit: Schools and Education

ACTIVITIES

1. Write a sentence to explain each of the following words.
   (a) lyre, **(b)** scroll, **(c)** knight, **(d)** ludi, **(e)** craftsman
2. **(a)** List the subjects that Roman children learned in school. **(b)** Compare them with the subjects that you learn in school. What has stayed the same? What is different?
3. Pair work: Look carefully at the Roman Numeral Table below. Write a Roman numeral and then cover the table. Can your partner tell you what number your Roman numeral stands for? Test each other with different Roman numerals!

Roman Numeral Table

1	I	11	XI	21	XXI	31	XXXI	200	CC	1700	MDCC
2	II	12	XII	22	XXII	40	XL	300	CCC	1800	MDCCC
3	III	13	XIII	23	XXIII	50	L	400	CD	1900	MCM
4	IV	14	XIV	24	XXIV	60	LX	500	D	2000	MM
5	V	15	XV	25	XXV	70	LXX	600	DC		
6	VI	16	XVI	26	XXVI	80	LXXX	700	DCC		
7	VII	17	XVII	27	XXVII	90	XC	800	DCCC		
8	VIII	18	XVIII	28	XXVIII	100	C	900	CM		
9	IX	19	IXX	29	IXXX	101	CI	1000	M		
10	X	20	XX	30	XXX	150	CL	1600	MDC		

Good Luck!

Early schools in Ireland

If you had lived in Ireland during the sixth century, you could have been educated at one of the great monasteries – but only if you were a boy!

During the eighteenth and nineteenth centuries in Ireland, the sons of chieftains and important people were sent away from home to live with and learn from other families. They left home when they were seven or eight years old. This was known as fostering. Fostering helped to create bonds of friendship between families. However, girls had to stay at home and learn needlework, cookery, housework and some reading and writing (if they were lucky).

Poor children in the eighteenth century were often taught in houses, barns and in the open air, when the weather was good. Those schools were called 'hedge schools'. Most of the children at that time spoke Irish, so the hedge school teachers taught them English, as well as Maths, Latin and History.

Strand: Continuity and Change Over Time   **Strand Unit:** Schools and Education

NATIONAL SCHOOLS BEGIN

National schools were first built in Ireland in 1831 AD. Both boys and girls were sent to national school. Children started in Junior Infants and they could stay in school for up to 10 years. The most senior class was 7th Class. As time went on, nuns, priests and brothers became very involved in the education of children. The first national schools were not as big or as comfortable as the schools of today. Many were very crowded. Sometimes the windows were so high that the pupils could not see outside. They had to keep all of their attention on their lessons. In many schools, children had to bring a sod of turf or a lump of coal to school each day, so that there would be enough fuel to keep the fire lighting.

School building from 1845

A classroom from 1845

NO COMFORTS!

In these national schools, pupils had to sit on benches with no backs, making them feel quite uncomfortable. Sometimes there were more than 100 children in one classroom! Some children were taught in a room known as a gallery. This was a type of classroom with stairs that ran across the width of the room. The pupils at the back were sitting higher up than those down in the front. Some children in Ireland had to work very hard at home and on the family farm before and after school each day. They had to walk long distances to and from school. There was no school-bus service and very few children had bicycles. One nice thing about some schools in the nineteenth century was that children got hot cocoa and bread at lunchtime! The older pupils prepared the lunch.

A gallery-style classroom from around 1900 AD

Strand: Continuity and Change Over Time   Strand Unit: Schools and Education

NATIONAL SCHOOLS OF THE PAST

The children who went to school in Ireland 100 years ago learned to read and write, just as they did in Ancient Greece and Rome. The children of 100 years ago often chanted their tables and their spellings. Sometimes pupils still do this. They also did arithmetic, or sums. They used slates and chalk when they were learning to write. As children improved at handwriting, they began to use nib pens and ink. Good handwriting was very important; it had to be clear and neat. The most beautiful type of handwriting was called 'copperplate'. Some teachers got very cross when pupils accidentally dripped blots of ink onto their copies. The pupils were punished if the teacher thought their work was messy.

School slate and chalk

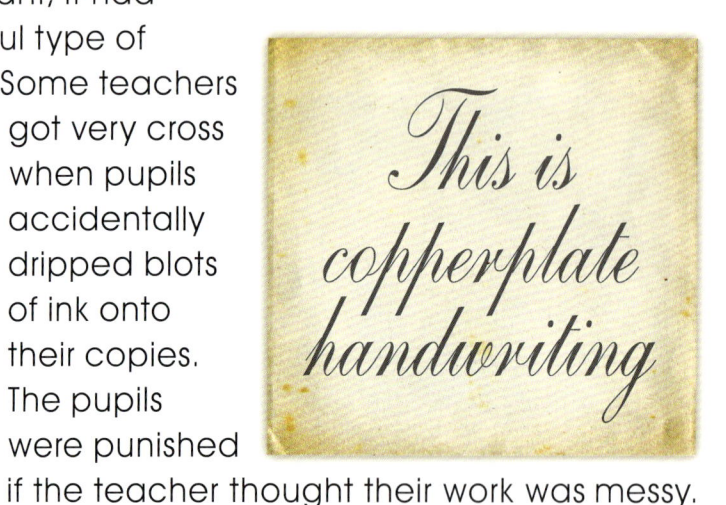

This is copperplate handwriting

Nib pen and ink

WHAT CHILDREN LEARNED 100 YEARS AGO

The children of 100 years ago learned many of the same subjects that you learn today. Their subjects included English, Irish, History, Geography and Nature Study. Girls were taught needlework. They made skirts and they knitted socks. Boys were sometimes taught woodwork. There was no PE back then, but children were taught 'Drill' in their classrooms or in the playground when the weather was good. Doing Drill meant that they had to stand in rows and move their arms and legs. They did exercises such as touching their toes, as the teacher called out commands. If you like art, you would have been disappointed by the schools of that time. There was only drawing, no painting.

Drill

One of the biggest differences between the schools in Ireland in the past and the schools of today is the way in which the children were taught. Like the schools of Ancient Greece and Rome, there was quite a lot of 'learning off by heart' to be done and there were not many books.

Strand: Continuity and Change Over Time   Strand Unit: Schools and Education

ACTIVITIES

A. Can You Remember?

1. How many years is it since national schools began in Ireland?
2. What activity did children do instead of PE?
3. What fuels were used to heat national schools in the past?
4. What name was given to sewing and knitting?
5. What did children in national school use for writing in the past?

B. Choose the Correct Answer to Complete Each Sentence.

1. Irish children were given _____ for lunch.
   A. soup, B. pizza, C. cocoa and bread, or D. sandwiches
2. National schools began in Ireland in _____.
   A. 1976, B. 1831, C. 2001, or D. 1842
3. Drill was a form of _____.
   A. writing, B. art, C. PE, or D. needlework
4. The most beautiful type of handwriting practised in old national schools was _____.
   A. silverplate, B. goldplate, C. copperplate, or D. bronzeplate

C. Think About It.

1. Imagine that an Irish boy or girl from 100 years ago could visit your classroom today. What would he/she be happy about? What might he/she miss?
2. Do you think that children are treated better now than they were in the past? Give reasons for your answer.
3. Why do you think girls had a lesser chance of being sent to school than boys had in the past?

D. Get Creative.

1. Invite an older person from your locality to come to your classroom. Write a list of questions and ask him/her to share memories of what life was like when he/she was at school.
2. Pair work: Examine the photograph of the schoolboys on page 57. Write a letter to one of the boys, explaining how your classroom differs from his. (For example, the classroom furniture that we use today and how it is arranged, our books, wall-charts, etc.)

E. Digging Deeper

The Celts used an alphabet called Ogham, which was made up of a series of lines and dots. Ogham words were written from top to bottom, as in the example on the right. Use the internet to have some fun with the Ogham Alphabet. Your teacher will give you a list of words to key into a search engine.

M
A
H
G
O

Strand: Continuity and Change Over Time   Strand Unit: Schools and Education   59

Unit 12: King Arthur and Excalibur

New Words
Camelot   Saxons   Excalibur

1 No one can be sure if King Arthur was a real king. Over the years, the stories about him have become legends. A legend can start off as a true story, but as it is told over and over, new bits are added. It becomes impossible to tell which bits are true and which are not! There are many legends about King Arthur. This is the legend about Arthur and the sword, Excalibur.

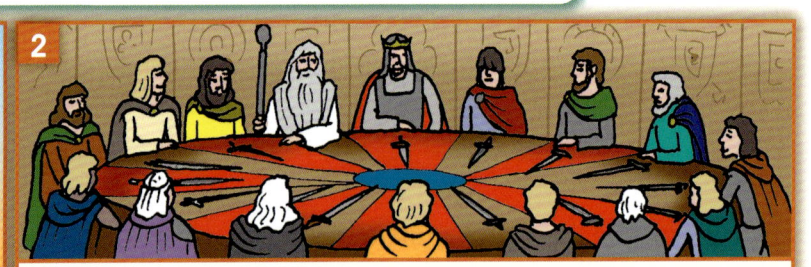

2 Soon after Arthur had been crowned King of England, he gathered a great army and got rid of the enemies of the country. Those enemies, the Saxons, had mostly come from Germany. Arthur gave back the lands that the Saxons had stolen from the English people. He built many castles to defend the coasts and borders of the kingdom. Afterwards, he sent for his most loyal followers and brought them all to live at his palace in Camelot. His famous army of knights also stayed in Camelot, protecting it from enemies. Arthur's knights were known as the 'Knights of the Round Table'. A very wise magician called Merlin always stayed by Arthur's side to help him in times of need.

3 Although Arthur had defeated the Saxons, he had a number of enemies among the English people. He had many battles to fight. After one very fierce battle, he was so weak that he could not climb up onto his horse. His sword was broken during the fighting. Merlin brought Arthur deep into the forest, to the cottage of an ancient healer. She treated Arthur's wounds with medicine. After three days, Arthur was rested and well enough to leave. They thanked the healer and rode away.

4 *I WISH I HADN'T BROKEN MY SWORD.*

SOON YOU'LL HAVE A SWORD THAT WILL LAST FOREVER. IT WILL BE THE BEST SWORD IN THE WORLD AND IT WILL COME FROM THE DEPTHS OF AVALON.

Avalon was a lake beside the forest. Arthur had no idea what Merlin was talking about, but he trusted him anyway. Merlin always seemed to know what was best.

Strand: Story   Strand Unit: Myths and Legends

5 They emerged from the shadows of the trees and into the bright sunshine. There before them, was Lake Avalon. Arthur gazed at the water's silvery surface. At the centre of the lake, a hand suddenly rose out of the water. It was grasping a sword covered in sparkling jewels!

LOOK OVER THERE! WHAT IS IT?

IT'S EXCALIBUR; THE SWORD YOU WILL CARRY UNTIL THE END OF YOUR DAYS.

6 Arthur jumped down from his horse and began to wade into the water. Suddenly, a tall woman glided across the surface of the water towards him.

THE LADY OF THE LAKE!

ARTHUR, EXCALIBUR WILL BE YOURS IF YOU DO AS I ASK.

I WILL DO WHATEVER IS IN MY POWER.

GET INTO MY BOAT AND ROW OUT TO THE MIDDLE OF THE LAKE.

7 Arthur raced along the shore. He stepped into the boat and rowed out to the centre of the lake. His heart was pounding as he reached out towards the sword with shaking fingers.

8 As soon as Arthur gripped the handle of the sword, the hand slid back down under the water. The Lady vanished and the lake was smooth and calm once more. Excalibur was the finest weapon that Arthur had ever seen.

I FEEL AS THOUGH I AM HOLDING MAGIC IN MY HAND. IS IT REALLY MINE?

IT'S YOURS FOR NOW, BUT A DAY WILL COME WHEN YOU WILL HAVE TO GIVE IT BACK.

Strand: Story Strand Unit: Myths and Legends

7.   With the help of Excalibur, Arthur won many battles and overcame many enemies. Years later, a great battle took place in Camlann, near Scotland. King Arthur's army was defeated. All of his knights were killed, except for Sir Bedivere.

10. Tears rolled down Sir Bedivere's cheeks as he laid Arthur down beside the lake.

THIS IS NO TIME FOR TEARS. I HAVE ONE MORE TASK FOR YOU BEFORE I DIE. TAKE EXCALIBUR AND THROW IT INTO THE LAKE. TELL ME WHAT HAPPENS.

9. Arthur was badly wounded in the battle and he asked Sir Bedivere to bring him to Lake Avalon.

11. Sir Bedivere thought it would be a waste to throw such a great sword into the lake, so he hid it in the reeds. He went back to Arthur and told him that he had thrown the sword into the water and that it had sunk with a splash.

YOU'RE LYING TO ME, SIR BEDIVERE. YOU HAVE BEEN MY GREAT FRIEND FOR SO MANY YEARS. PLEASE DO AS I WISH NOW.

12. Filled with shame, Sir Bedivere did as he was asked. He flung Excalibur way out into the lake. A hand rose out of the water and grasped it by the handle. The hand held the sword there for a moment, before sliding back down under the water.

Sir Bedivere went back and told his king that all was well. Arthur closed his eyes and smiled peacefully.

13. When Arthur opened his eyes again, Sir Bedivere gently placed him inside a boat.

The boat drifted towards the centre of the lake and disappeared into the mist.

62   Strand: Story   Strand Unit: Myths and Legends

ACTIVITIES

A. Can You Remember?

1. What is a legend?
2. What did Arthur do after he was crowned king?
3. What were Arthur's knights called?
4. Who was Merlin?
5. Where did Merlin bring Arthur after the fierce battle?

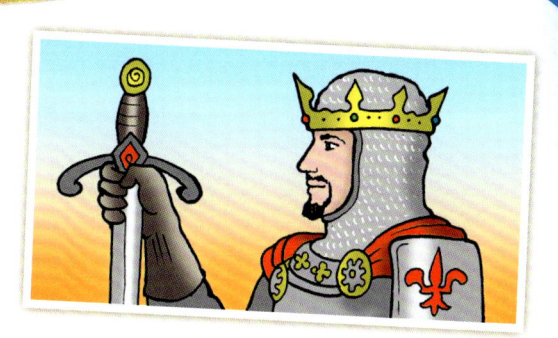

B. Choose the Correct Answer to Complete Each Sentence.

1. The Knights of the Round Table protected _____.
   A. London, **B.** Camelot, **C.** Lake Avalon, or **D.** the forest
2. Excalibur was found in _____.
   A. a lake, **B.** a river, **C.** the sea, or **D.** Scotland
3. Merlin brought Arthur into the woods to _____.
   A. escape, **B.** fight, **C.** hide, or **D.** rest
4. The Saxons came from _____.
   A. Camelot, **B.** Camlan, **C.** Germany, or **D.** England

C. Think About It.

1. Do you think that Sir Bedivere was a loyal knight? Give a reason for your answer.
2. Why do you think the Lady of the Lake wanted Arthur to do what she asked?
3. Why do you think Arthur wanted the sword to be thrown back into the lake?
4. Do you think that Arthur was a powerful king?
5. How do you think Arthur lost the final battle?

D. Get Creative.

1. If you had been at Lake Avalon, what would you have done when you saw the hand rising up out of the water?
2. Write what Sir Bedivere must have been thinking when he saw the sword disappearing into the water.
3. Rewrite the legend of King Arthur in your own words. Draw pictures for your text.

E. Digging Deeper

1. Read the book, *Tales of King Arthur: King Arthur and the Round Table* by Hudson Talbot (Harper Collins).
2. Use the internet to learn more about King Arthur. Your teacher will give you a list of words to key into a search engine.

Unit 13: Life in Norman Ireland

New Words
mail   motte and bailey   drawbridge   dungeon   goblet   minstrels   battlements

Timeline

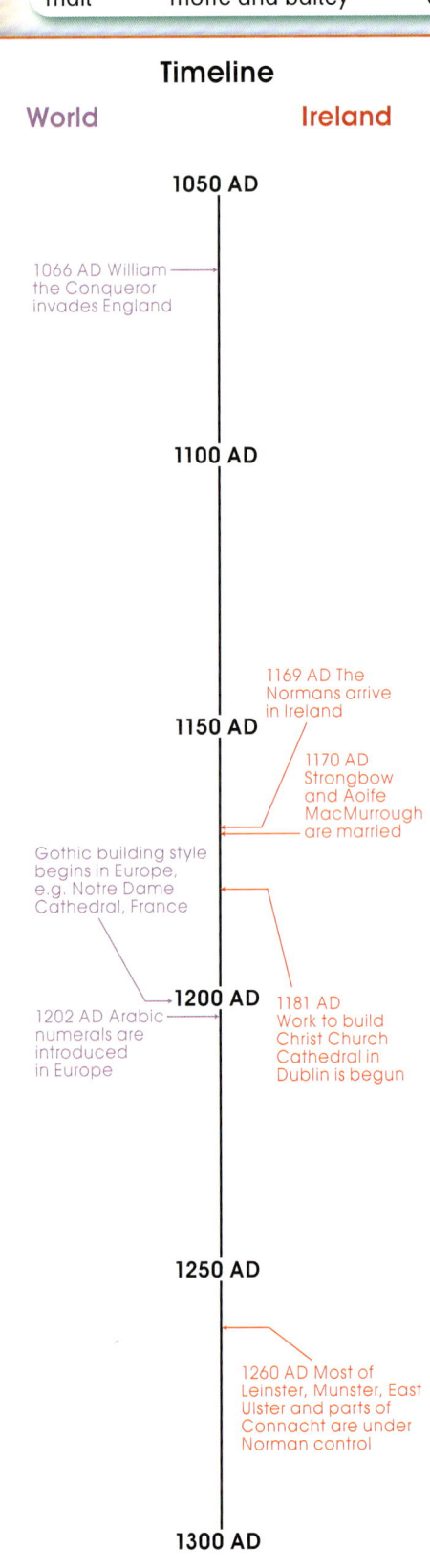

World | **Ireland**

- 1050 AD
- 1066 AD William the Conqueror invades England
- 1100 AD
- 1150 AD
- 1169 AD The Normans arrive in Ireland
- 1170 AD Strongbow and Aoife MacMurrough are married
- Gothic building style begins in Europe, e.g. Notre Dame Cathedral, France
- 1200 AD
- 1181 AD Work to build Christ Church Cathedral in Dublin is begun
- 1202 AD Arabic numerals are introduced in Europe
- 1250 AD
- 1260 AD Most of Leinster, Munster, East Ulster and parts of Connacht are under Norman control
- 1300 AD

Who were the Normans?

Around 1000 AD, some of the Vikings who had been raiding France were given permission by the French king to settle down and live in France. These Viking settlers became known as the Normans. The area of France where they lived is called Normandy, which means 'land of the North men'. The Normans were very well-trained soldiers. The knights were the most important soldiers in their army. The most famous leader of the Normans was William, Duke of Normandy. He was also known as 'William the Conqueror', because of his successful attack on England in 1066 AD.

Norman knights

Knights wore helmets and coats of mail. The mail was made from thousands of rings of metal that were linked together. It helped to protect the knight's body, as did the kite-shaped shield that he carried. Very often, the knight's coat of arms was painted on his shield. His weapons were a lance (spear), a sword and a battle-axe. Knights had another advantage over their enemies: they fought on horseback. Their saddles were fitted with stirrups to keep their feet secure. This made it very difficult for their enemies to knock them off their horses. Archers walked behind the knights in battle and protected them with their bows and arrows.

Strand: Life, Society, Work and Culture in the Past   Strand Unit: Life in Norman Ireland

Why the Normans came to Ireland

Diarmuid MacMurrough was born in 1110 AD and he died in 1171 AD. Diarmuid was King of Leinster, but he did not get on with Ruairí O'Connor, the High King of Ireland. Because of this, Diarmuid lost his kingship. He had no friends in Ireland to support him against the High King, so he decided to look elsewhere for help. The Normans had attacked and conquered England in 1066 AD and they went on to conquer Wales. There were many Norman lords living in Wales, so Diarmuid travelled there to see if they would help him. He promised that if they helped him to win back his kingdom, he would give them lands in Ireland. Diarmuid made two special promises to a Norman called Richard de Clare. Richard was known as 'Strongbow', because he was very skilled with a type of bow that was long and strong. Diarmuid promised Strongbow that he would give him his daughter, Aoife, in marriage. Diarmuid's second promise was that after his death, Strongbow would become King of Leinster.

Caerphilly Castle, Wales home of the de Clares

Arrival of the Normans

In May of 1169 AD, a group of about 600 Normans, led by Robert Fitzstephen, landed at Bannow Bay in County Wexford. Very quickly, they captured Wexford Town. The following year, a Norman chief called Raymond le Gros landed at Baginbun in County Wexford. He brought with him an even larger group of Normans. The rhyme, 'At the creek of Baginbun, Ireland was lost and won' comes from the battle that took place between the Normans and the Irish. Strongbow arrived a month later and he captured the county of Waterford. He married Aoife, the daughter of Diarmuid MacMurrough, the following day. The Normans then marched north through Leinster. The High King sent out an army to cut them off, but Diarmuid showed the Normans a way through the Dublin Mountains. They marched through Rathfarnham and they kept going until they reached the walls of Dublin. Raymond le Gros attacked the city and captured it.

From *The Marriage of Princess Aoife of Leinster with the Norman Richard de Clare (Strongbow)*, 1854

Buildings

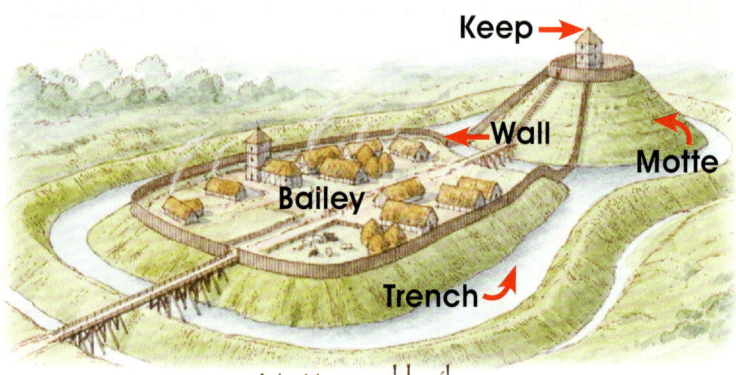

As well as being good soldiers, the Normans were excellent builders. After they won a battle, they usually built a castle on the land that they had taken. They had to work quickly in case of further attacks, so they used earth and timber to build a defence known as a motte and bailey. First, they dug a large trench. The soil from the trench was piled up to make a large hill, or mound, which they called a 'motte'.

Motte and bailey

On top of the motte, they built a wooden or stone tower called a 'keep'. Then they built a wooden wall around the whole structure. The area inside the wall was called the 'bailey'. This is where they built their houses. The trench around the motte and bailey was filled with water. If the bailey was attacked, the Normans would retreat to the tower on the motte. They could defend themselves well from there. Examples of mottes can still be seen in Ireland.

Motte and bailey, Clough, County Down

Norman castles

Later on, in the thirteenth and fourteenth centuries, the Normans built stone castles that were much stronger than their earlier ones. The walls were very high and up to 6 m thick, to protect the lord and his family. The walls were also surrounded by a moat filled with water. To get into the castle, people had to cross over the moat by drawbridge. The soldiers wound the drawbridge up or down, in order to let friends in and keep enemies out. Inside the castle, there were several floors, or levels. The dungeon, where prisoners were kept, was on the lowest level. On the next level, there was a chapel and a guards' room. Above this, there was a great hall, where the lord, his family and their visitors dined. The bedrooms were above the great hall. On the very top of the castle, was a place known as the battlements, where soldiers kept a lookout over the surrounding countryside.

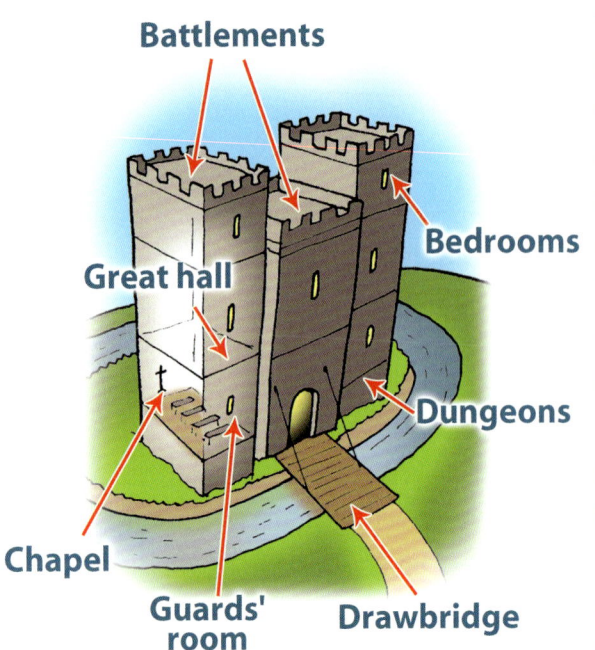

A Norman lord and his family usually ate two meals each day; one in the morning and one in the evening. They had plates for their food and knives for cutting meat, but they used their fingers instead of forks. Wine was served in goblets, which looked like wine glasses made from metal. The kitchens were outside in the grounds of the castle. Cooked food had to be carried a long way, so it was often cold by the time it reached the table! Musicians known as minstrels played music and sang to entertain guests. They played wooden flutes, recorders and lyres. Examples of Norman castles are Trim Castle, County Meath, and King John's Castle, Limerick.

Goblet

Trim Castle, County Meath

King John's Castle, Limerick

Food and farming

The Normans ate bread made from wheat or oats. They also made porridge from oats. Their vegetables were peas, beans, leeks and onions. On special occasions such as festival days, they had beef, mutton and pork. Those who lived near rivers or the sea caught fish. They usually drank water or milk and sometimes they had ale brewed from barley. Large amounts of oats and wheat were grown so that some could be sold, or exported, to England and France. Lots of sheep were raised, too, and huge amounts of wool were sold abroad.

Clothes

Wealthy people wore clothes made from linen and fine wool. Lords wore long gowns with wide sleeves. They also had short jackets, belted and trimmed with fur. Their stockings (called hose) were coloured. Ladies wore long dresses tied at the waist with jewelled belts. Their cloaks were tied at the neck with a chain or cord. Both men and women wore pointed shoes made of leather. The children dressed just like adults. Poorer people wore clothes made from a rougher woollen material. Women's dresses were long. Men wore tunics and leggings. Wooden clogs or shoes made from cloth were worn by the adults, but children usually went barefoot.

Wealthy couple

Poor couple

Hot History

The Normans 'dry-cleaned' their clothes by hanging them in the garderobe, which was a room with toilets. They believed that the smell would kill any lice that lived in their clothes! Ugh!

Strand: Life, Society, Work and Culture in the Past   Strand Unit: Life in Norman Ireland

Amusements and festivals

People who lived in Norman times had to work hard. The children of poorer people had to work in the kitchen, mind farm animals, make clothes and look after the gardens. When their work was done, they had time to play games like Hide and Seek and Blind Man's Bluff. The children of the rich lords had toy soldiers, wooden horses and dolls to play with. Chess and draughts were popular games, too. In the evenings, both children and adults listened to storytelling, poetry and songs. The Norman settlers took on the Irish traditions and customs. Sundays and Church holidays were days of rest. There were also special festival days. For example, Saint Brigid's Day, on February 1st, marked the beginning of spring. May Day, or Lá Bealtaine, marked the beginning of summer. Lughnasa, on August 1st, was very popular, as it was the beginning of the harvest. Samhain (Hallowe'en), on October 31st, was another important festival. On those special days, games and competitions were held in villages, with people playing bowls and skittles. They also liked to show off their skills as archers and wrestlers. Hurling was very popular, but it was a much rougher and more dangerous game than it is now.

Celebrating a win in archery

The Normans and the Irish

Music and dancing

When the Normans first came to Ireland, they spoke French and had their own customs. Over time, they married Irish people and their children spoke Irish. They dressed like their Irish neighbours, in tunics of linen and cloaks of wool. While the Irish had always enjoyed music, songs and poetry, the Normans loved dancing. Eventually, both music and dancing became very popular with all of the people. Some Normans let their hair grow long and grew moustaches in the style of the Irish men. They also began to ride their horses bareback (without using saddles) like the Irish. In many ways, the Normans became 'more Irish than the Irish themselves'!

Strand: Life, Society, Work and Culture in the Past   **Strand Unit:** Life in Norman Ireland

ACTIVITIES

A. Can You Remember?

1. In what year did the Normans first arrive in Ireland?
2. When did Aoife marry Strongbow?
3. What was Strongbow's full name?
4. Write three things that made the Norman knights successful in battle.
5. What language was spoken by the Normans when they first came to Ireland?

B. Choose the Correct Answer to Complete Each Sentence.

1. Diarmuid MacMurrough came from _____.
   A. Ireland, B. Wales, C. France, or D. England
2. The _____ was not a weapon used by the Normans.
   A. sword, B. lance, C. rifle, or D. battle-axe
3. Aoife was Diarmuid MacMurrough's _____.
   A. mother, B. cousin, C. sister, or D. daughter
4. The Norman coat of mail was made from _____.
   A. cloth, B. wood, C. metal, or D. plastic

C. Think About It.

1. What do you think of Diarmuid MacMurrough? Do you think he would be a good friend? Give reasons for your answer.
2. Use your atlas: The Normans travelled north from Waterford to Dublin. What route might they have taken and what towns might they have passed through?
3. How could you tell from a Norman's clothes whether he/she was wealthy or poor?

D. Get Creative.

1. Pair work: Act out the conversation between Aoife and her father when he told her that she was to marry Strongbow.
2. Imagine that you are a young Norman knight who fought in the battle at Wexford. Write a letter to your parents telling them about the battle. For example, tell them about your coat of mail and how it helped you in battle.

E. Digging Deeper

1. Use the internet or the library to find out where Strongbow is buried.
2. Write out a Norman shopping list using Roman numerals. (Tip: '4 leeks' is 'IV leeks'.)
3. Use the internet to find out some really interesting information about the Normans. Your teacher will give you a list of words to key into a search engine.

Unit 14: Life in Medieval Towns

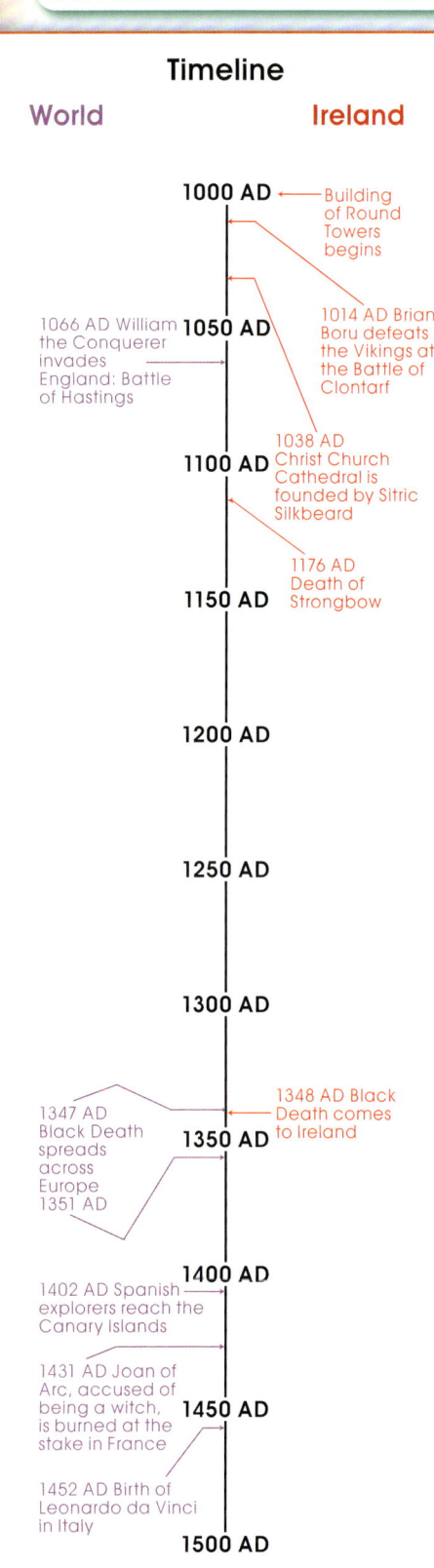

New Words
town crier   toll   guild   stocks   plague

Timeline

World | **Ireland**

- 1000 AD — Building of Round Towers begins
- 1014 AD Brian Boru defeats the Vikings at the Battle of Clontarf
- 1038 AD Christ Church Cathedral is founded by Sitric Silkbeard
- 1066 AD William the Conquerer invades England: Battle of Hastings
- 1176 AD Death of Strongbow
- 1347 AD Black Death spreads across Europe 1351 AD
- 1348 AD Black Death comes to Ireland
- 1402 AD Spanish explorers reach the Canary Islands
- 1431 AD Joan of Arc, accused of being a witch, is burned at the stake in France
- 1452 AD Birth of Leonardo da Vinci in Italy

Medieval Homes

After the Normans came to Ireland in 1169 AD, more people began to live in villages and towns. Houses were built close together and they could be any shape or size. People did not need permission to make their houses bigger, so they just built as they pleased. Houses were often made of wood. As many of them had thatched roofs, people were always afraid that their roofs would catch fire. For safety, they kept a leather fire-bucket full of water. Some houses also had a long hook hanging outside. The hook was used to pull the burning thatch off the roof, in order to stop the fire from spreading.

Roofs on fire

Dirty Old Town!

The streets of a medieval town were very narrow and very dirty. There were no bin collections. Instead, there were gutters running down the middle of the streets, where people just threw their rubbish. The gutters were full of rotten food, dead cats and dogs, sewage, dirty water and any other unpleasant thing that you can think of! The smell must have been awful. People often held handkerchiefs to their noses as they walked through the filthy streets. However, there was one group of creatures that loved the gutters: rats! They were seen everywhere, rummaging through rubbish.

Strand: Life, Society, Work and Culture in the Past **Strand Unit:** Life in Medieval Towns and Countryside in Ireland and Europe

CLUES TO THE PAST

Some medieval towns were surrounded by high walls, with gates that were locked at sunset each evening. The walls kept the townspeople safe. Medieval town walls and gates can still be seen in many places around Ireland. Streetnames also give us clues, like 'Sráid an Dá Gheata' or 'the street of the two gates', in Dingle, County Kerry. Streets were also named after the activities of medieval times. Those names are still used in Dublin City to this day; for example, Cornmarket and Haymarket were market areas. Streets were also named after the buildings of the time; for example, Abbey Street was named after Saint Mary's Abbey (a monastery) and Mill Street and Windmill Lane were named after grain mills.

Water Gate, Youghal, County Cork

Hot History
Medieval times (or the Middle Ages) began around 500 AD and went on until almost 1500 AD.

Fethard Village walls, County Tipperary

LIFE IN THE TOWNS

Religion was very important to medieval people and they always went to church on Sundays and holy days. There was at least one church in every town. Many towns had a market square, where people came to buy and sell goods. There were no newspapers, radios or televisions, but there was a town crier, who rang a bell to let people know that he had news to tell. A few towns in Ireland had a town crier up until the 1950s.

Town crier

Hot History
People who broke the rules were punished by having their legs (and sometimes their head or arms) put in the stocks. People jeered them and threw rotten eggs or other nasty things at them.

Some people had a little patch of ground beside their house or outside the walls of the town, where they grew vegetables for their family. If you wanted to go into the town, you had to enter through the gates. Visitors were charged a fee, or toll, to pass through the gates. This was a good way for the mayor and the town councillors to collect money. They used the money to build better walls and to repair the streets when they got damaged. Each town had its own rules and laws that had to be obeyed.

Strand: Life, Society, Work and Culture in the Past Strand Unit: Life in Medieval Towns and Countryside in Ireland and Europe

MEDIEVAL SHOPS

COME FOR A GREAT DAY'S SHOPPING IN OUR MEDIEVAL TOWN!

Medieval shops were quite small and their windows had no glass. The shopkeepers often made the goods that they sold. They usually lived in rooms above their shops. Each morning, they displayed the items for sale by placing them on stalls outside the shop doors. Craftsmen usually hung signs outside their shops to show people what was for sale. A sign might have a picture of a fish, knives or gloves, depending on the owner's craft. Most people could not read, so there was no point in writing words above the shops. People who made the same kind of objects or crafts set up clubs together, known as guilds. The members of a guild usually lived on the same street; for example, in Dublin there is Cook Street and Weavers' Square. The guild members also had meetings, where they talked about any problems that they had. Sometimes they collected money to help the widows and children of members who had died.

Hot History

Get the latest fashion in medieval men's shoes! Handmade with real leather, these comfortable shoes are flat with no heels. The long, pointed toes come stuffed with moss to keep them in shape. Try them!

ACTIVITIES

1. Write a sentence to explain each of the words and phrases listed below.
   (a) town walls, **(b)** craftsman, **(c)** town crier, **(d)** toll
2. Pair work: *People who lived in medieval towns had an easier life than we have today.* Do you agree or disagree? Discuss it with your partner and then write your answer.
3. Explain what a guild was and what its members did.

MEDIEVAL FAIRS

During medieval times, people had their own forms of entertainment. Fair days were held in many towns and lots of different types of people attended them. Farmers travelled long distances to buy and sell cattle, sheep and pigs. Traders came carrying their goods on packhorses. They set up stalls selling items that people needed for their homes. Among the crowd were nobles dressed in silk, as well as thieves and beggars. There were many interesting things to see and buy. Cheeses, wool, leather goods and wine were common. It was sometimes possible to find oranges and beautiful materials like silk and velvet from far away countries.

Medieval fair, 1400s

Strand: Life, Society, Work and Culture in the Past   **Strand Unit:** Life in Medieval Towns and Countryside in Ireland and Europe

Entertainment

Sword swallowers, jugglers, mummers (travelling actors) and musicians entertained people at the fairs. Some fairs also had a dancing bear. (Medieval people did not really think about animal rights.) Children loved the fair days, because they often got special treats like fruit or tarts. As most people could not read at this time, the priests allowed mummers to perform stories from the Bible in the churches. The miracle plays, which you read about in Unit 6, were acted on carts that were wheeled around the towns. In Ireland, men and boys liked to play hurling, but it had to be stopped, because people were often hurt or killed. Handball was played and dancing, chess and draughts were also popular. Children liked to play Blind Man's Bluff, Piggy-back and a game like bowling that was called Ninepins. They also played with spinning tops and marbles.

Children's Games, painted in 1560

Page from the Gutenberg Bible

The printing press

The printing press was invented in 1440 AD by Johann Gutenberg in Germany. For the first time ever, books could be printed quickly and they were cheaper to buy. More people learned to read, so news and information about politics, religion, science and other topics spread faster than ever before. The first book to be printed by Gutenberg was the Bible. Some people say that Gutenberg's printing press was the most important invention of the second millennium. ('Millennium' means a thousand years.)

A DEADLY PLAGUE

A deadly plague known as the Black Death caused great hardship when it arrived in Europe in 1347 AD. Historians tell us that up to half of the people who lived in Europe at the time died. The disease was carried by rats from the great sailing ships that were travelling round the world. It spread to humans when they were bitten by the fleas that lived in the rats' fur. People knew they had caught the plague when they saw red rings on their bodies, followed by big black spots under their arms, behind their knees and on their necks. There was no cure for the disease, so people who caught the plague knew there was little hope of surviving.

Illustration of plague victims, 1300s

Ring-a-Ring o'Rosy

The rhyme 'Ring-a-Ring o'Rosy' was about the plague. See how this verse matches the disease:

Ring-a-ring o'rosy	➡ Red rings on your body
A pocket full of posies	➡ Flowers and herbs in your pocket
A-tishoo! A-tishoo!	➡ Sneezing
We all fall down!	➡ Death

Hot History

Doctors at this time did not realise that being clean helped to stop infections from spreading. They were proud of their bloody aprons. They often kept a bird in the room where they performed operations, because they thought it brought good luck.

SPREAD OF THE PLAGUE

The plague spread very quickly in cities, because they were dirty and overcrowded. A lot of people did not have enough food to eat, so they were not strong enough to resist the disease. Dublin, Drogheda, Dundalk, Waterford and Kilkenny were the worst affected towns in Ireland. Whole families died there. People who lived in the countryside were much safer from the disease. When the plague victims died, their bodies were burned. The smell was very bad. Some people carried herbs and flowers in their pockets to lessen the smell. They also thought that this would protect them from the disease.

Illustration of plague victims, 1503

ACTIVITIES

A. Can You Remember?

1. How did Cornmarket and Windmill Lane get their names?
2. Who invented the printing press?
3. Name two towns in Ireland where people died from the plague.
4. Why was Joan of Arc burned at the stake? (Hint: Look at the timeline.)
5. When did the Black Death come to Europe and how was it spread?

B. Choose the Correct Answer to Complete Each Sentence.

1. A guild was a club for _____.
   A. town criers, B. mayors, C. craftsmen, or D. nobles
2. People who broke the town rules were put in _____.
   A. stocks, B. plays, C. the town walls, or D. sailing ships
3. The Normans came to Ireland in _____.
   A. 119 AD, B. 1169 BC, C. 1196 AD, or D. 1169 AD
4. Visitors to gated towns had to pay a _____.
   A. town crier, B. toll, C. mummer, or D. guild

C. Think About It.

1. Who do you think had the job of making the laws in medieval towns and villages?
2. Do you know of any street in your town that may have been named in medieval times?
3. Can you think of any reason why the people in towns suffered more from the plague than the people who lived in the countryside?
4. Pair work: *Gutenberg's printing press was the most important invention of the second millennium.* Do you agree or disagree? Discuss it with your partner and then write your answer.

D. Get Creative.

1. Group work: Choose a trade or a craft for a medieval shop. Make a sign to put outside your shop. Remember to use symbols that people will recognise.
2. Imagine that you are a child living in a medieval town. All of your work is finished for the day. It is raining heavily, so you must stay at home. What will you and your brothers and sisters do to entertain yourselves for the evening?

E. Digging Deeper

Use the internet or the library to find out about one of the famous people listed below. Do a mini-project and present your findings to the class.
Joan of Arc,   Brian Boru,   William Tell,   William Wallace

Strand: Life, Society, Work and Culture in the Past   Strand Unit: Life in Medieval Towns and Countryside in Ireland and Europe

Unit 15: Christopher Columbus

New Words
seaport — crew — shipwrecked

Timeline

World | **Ireland**

1 AD

438 AD Saint Brendan is born

500 AD

1402 AD Spanish explorers reach the Canary Islands

1451 AD Christopher Columbus is born in Genoa, Italy

1484 AD Columbus asks the King and Queen of Spain for ships

1000 AD

1500 AD

1492 AD *Niña*, *Pinta* and *Santa Maria* set sail from Spain; Columbus arrives in the continent of America

1589 AD The potato comes to Ireland

1766 AD The turkey is brought to Europe from America

2000 AD

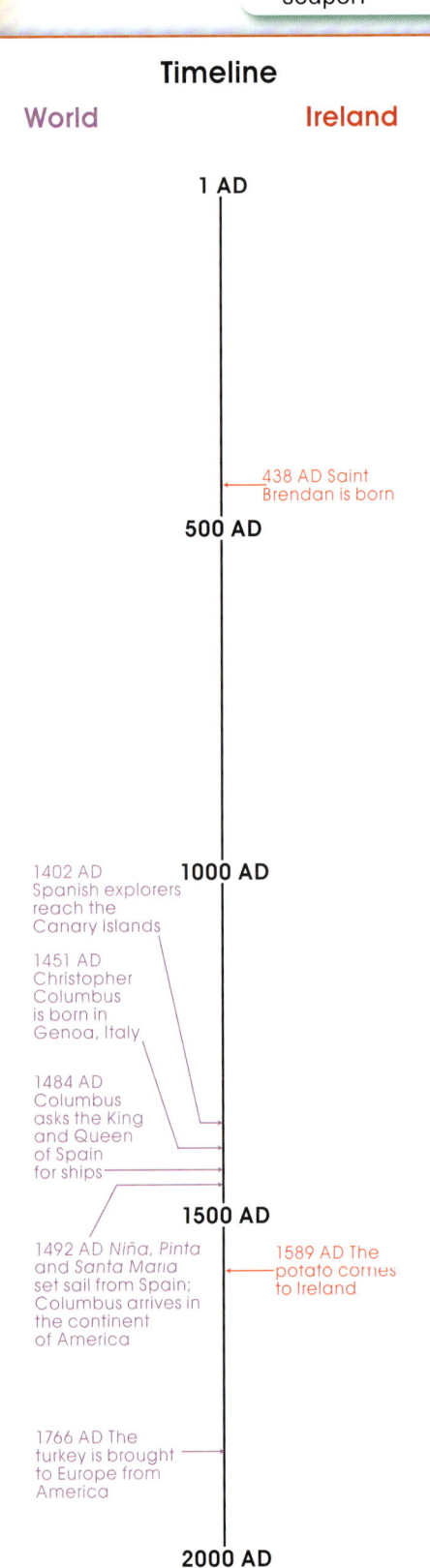

1
Christopher Columbus was born in Genoa in Italy, in 1451 AD. Genoa was a very busy seaport. He loved sailing and the sea. He longed to be a captain of his own ship some day. He made many sea voyages and in 1477, he went to live in Portugal. He sailed on Portuguese ships for a number of years.

2
At that time, many people thought the Earth was flat. They believed that a ship could fall off the edge of the world if it sailed too far! Columbus was sure that the Earth was round and that if you sailed west, you would finally end up in the east.

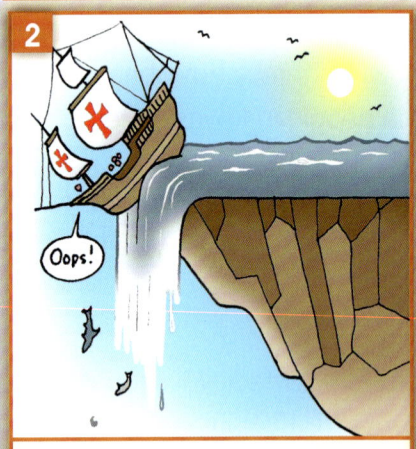

3
For years, the Portuguese had been exploring the coast of Africa. They were trying to find a different way of getting to India and China.

76 Strand: Story Strand Unit: Stories From the Lives of People in the Past

4

Columbus believed that there was nothing but sea between Europe and Asia and that he could get to India by sailing west instead of east. He was sure that by sailing west, he would travel all the way around the world until he eventually reached India. He hoped to find lots of gold and spices in India.

5

He needed money to buy ships and supplies in order to sail to India. He asked the Portuguese King for help, but he refused. In 1484, Columbus went to Spain and the King and Queen of Spain said that they would help him. They hoped that he would bring them back gold and other riches. He bought three ships: the *Niña*, the *Pinta* and the *Santa Maria*. However, he found it difficult to get sailors for his ships. Most sailors were afraid of falling off the edge of the world!

6

At last, he managed to find enough men who were willing to sail with him. Most of them were from small villages and towns in Spain. In August, 1492, Columbus set sail from Spain with a crew of 90 men. Five days later, they reached the Canary Islands. On September 6th, 1492, they headed west to cross the Atlantic. During their journey, the ships ran into many storms. After sailing without sight of land for 32 days, the sailors were worried and scared. They wanted to return to Spain while they still had enough food and drink to get them there.

Strand: Story   Strand Unit: Stories From the Lives of People in the Past

7 The following shows what Christopher Columbus might have written in his diary.

October 1, 1492

This is killing me! Where is land? We have sailed for days and days and there has been no sight of land. We have had clear skies and steady winds, but my crew is angry and they are fighting. There is talk of turning back. The crew has even threatened to push me overboard and sail back to Spain. I am not letting that happen. I have come too far to turn back now. Land must be near, I know it. Crewmen have spotted branches in the waters and birds that could not possibly go very far from land. From these signs, I am sure that land is near.

8 LAND AHOY!

He talked to his men and they agreed to continue on for just a few more days. On October 11th, 1492, they suddenly saw flocks of birds flying above the ship. They also saw seaweed and branches from trees floating in the water. A short while later, they saw land. Columbus and his men were happy and relieved.

9 They thought they had found the Indies, which is where India and China are today. They were wrong; they had actually landed on the coast of the Bahamas. They did not realise that they had arrived in a new continent. The new continent was America. As they drew near the shore the next morning, they saw a sandy beach with tall palm trees. Because Columbus thought this was the Indies, he called the people he met 'Indians' and he called the islands the 'West Indies'.

10 The people of the islands gave a warm welcome to the sailors. Columbus travelled around the islands in search of gold. In January, 1493, he and some of his crew sailed back to Spain aboard the *Niña* and the *Pinta*. The *Santa Maria* had been shipwrecked in a storm. He left 40 of his crew behind, promising to return for them in a year. He and his crew landed in Spain in March 1493. From there, they travelled to see the king and queen in Barcelona. There were great celebrations to welcome him home. He sailed to the West Indies three more times, but he always believed that he was sailing to India and China.

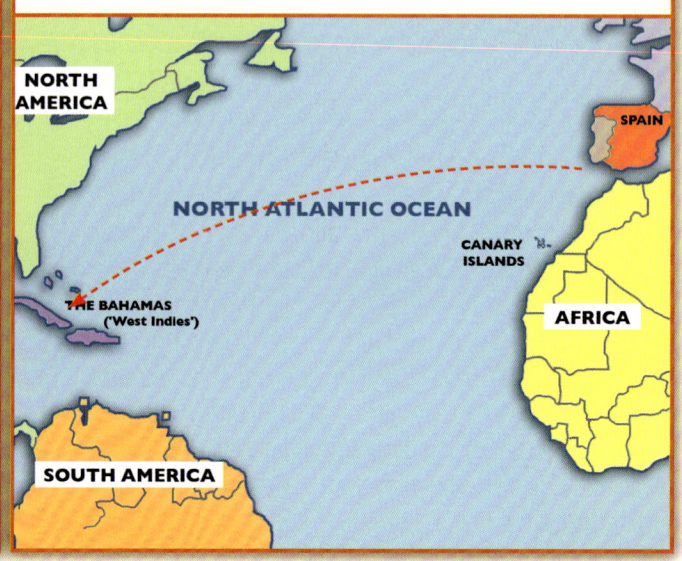

Strand: Story Strand Unit: Stories From the Lives of People in the Past

ACTIVITIES

A. Can You Remember?

1. In which Italian city was Columbus born?
2. Who gave Columbus the money to buy his ships?
3. What were the names of Columbus's three ships?
4. What did the King and Queen of Spain want Columbus to bring back for them?
5. Why was it difficult for Columbus to find sailors for his ships?

B. Choose the Correct Answer to Complete Each Sentence.

1. Columbus' ships reached the Canary Islands after _____.
   A. six days, B. a week, C. five days, or D. five weeks
2. For 32 days, they sailed without sight of _____.
   A. land, B. water, C. rain, or D. storms
3. Columbus was born in _____.
   A. 1415 AD, B. 141 BC, C. 1451 AD, or D. 1451 BC
4. In October 1492, Columbus and his sailors reached _____.
   A. India, B. the Bahamas, C. China, or D. Genoa

C. Think About It.

1. Do you think the crew had faith in Columbus? Give a reason for your answer.
2. Why do you think the islanders welcomed Columbus and his crew?
3. Why do you think Columbus returned three times to the West Indies?
4. What kind of person do you think Columbus was?
5. Having read about Saint Brendan, who do you think was the first European to arrive in America?

D. Get Creative.

1. Write a diary entry for Columbus on the first day of the voyage in August, 1492. Remember: Although he had his own ships, he had a crew of 90 men who believed that the Earth was flat!
2. Write the conversation between Columbus and the king and queen when he returned to Spain in March 1493.
3. If you were one of the sailors who was left behind on the island, how would you have spent your time?

E. Digging Deeper

Use the internet to learn more about Christopher Columbus. Your teacher will give you a list of words to key into a search engine.

Strand: Story   Strand Unit: Stories From the Lives of People in the Past

Unit 16: Transport

New Words

horsepower   penny-farthing   Tube   Métro   maglev   currach   Galway hooker   coffin ship
cargo   DART   Luas

Timeline

World | **Ireland**

1700 AD

1700s AD Steam engine is built by James Watt, Scotland

1750 AD

1776 AD Galway hookers begin to be used

1800 AD
1815 AD Bianconi Coaches provide first public transport system in Ireland

1834 AD Ireland's first railway from Dublin City to Dún Laoghaire is opened

1850 AD
1880s AD Petrol-driven car is invented by Daimler, Germany

1848 AD The Jeanie Johnson sails from Ireland to Canada

1900 AD
1903 AD First aeroplane flight by Wright Brothers, USA

1930 AD Amy Johnson is the first woman to fly solo from Britain to Australia

1950 AD
1961 AD Yuri Gagarin, Russia, is the first man in space

1958 AD First transatlantic flight service from Ireland to America

1969 AD Neil Armstrong, USA, is the first man to walk on the moon

2000 AD

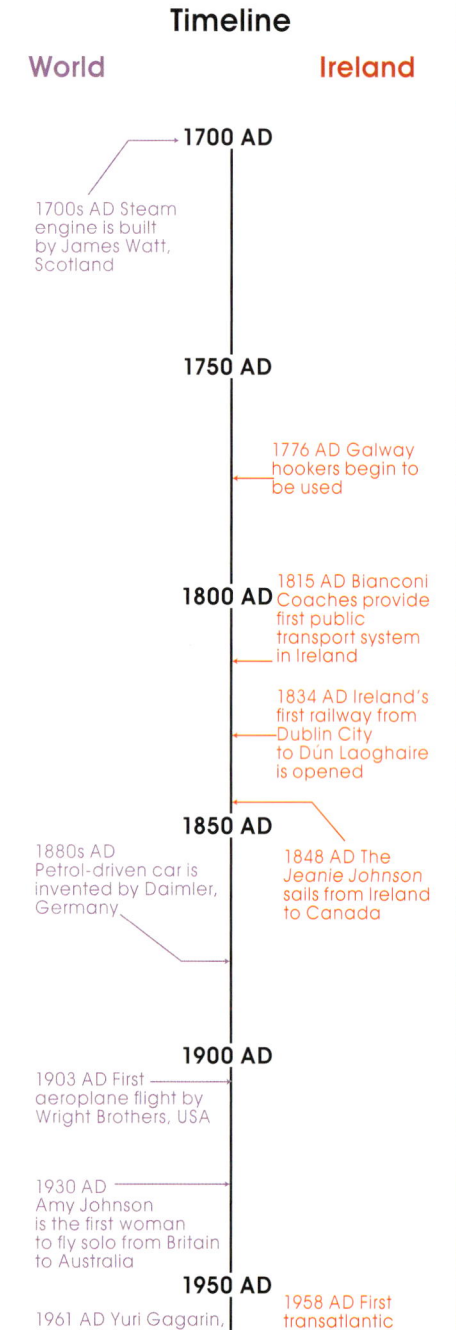

THE WHEEL

Thousands of years ago, the only way that people could get from one place to another was by walking. If they were moving to a new home, they had to carry everything by themselves. One day, a clever person decided that it would make more sense to use animals to carry goods. By 2000 BC, the wheel had been invented and life became much easier. Heavy loads could be transported farther and more easily. Horses, dogs, oxen and donkeys were used for thousands of years to transport people and goods. Ploughs, carts, wagons and carriages were all pulled by some kind of four-legged creature. The size and style of those vehicles changed over the years.

Ox-drawn wagon

HORSES

Horses were so important for transporting loads, that people's wealth began to be measured by the number of horses that they owned. Teams of horses were used for ploughing and harvesting and for pulling wagons and coaches. The power of a car's engine is still measured in horsepower to this day! The greater the horsepower, the faster the car. Charles Bianconi started a wonderful system of public transport in Ireland in 1815 AD. He used horse-drawn carriages, known as Bianconi Coaches, to carry passengers and to deliver post throughout the country.

Bianconi Coach

Strand: Continuity and Change Over Time   Strand Unit: Transport

Bicycles

In the late 1700s AD, the first bicycle was invented. Early bicycles, like the penny-farthing, were very different to the bikes we use now. They were probably quite difficult to ride and they did not go very fast. By 1885, an engine was developed that could be fitted onto a bicycle and so the first motorbike was born. Bicycles and motorbikes have changed so much since then, that someone who lived in the 1880s would hardly recognise them.

Penny-farthing bicycles

Hot History
The first motorcycle was built in Germany in 1885. It had a petrol engine and it was made from wood!

Cars

The first cars were invented in the 1880s. They were very difficult to get started and even more difficult to stop! Cars were thought to be so dangerous, that a man had to walk in front of them waving a red flag to warn people of on-coming traffic! Because the early cars had no roofs, people had to dress warmly to protect themselves from the weather and the dirt of the roads. They also wore goggles to protect their eyes. Only rich people could afford to buy cars, as they were very expensive to make and run.

A Benz car from 1894

Hot History
Up until the 1980s, lead was added to petrol to improve it. Lead is poisonous and dangerous to our health. It also caused serious pollution. Most cars can now use unleaded petrol.

Trams and buses

As towns and cities grew, more people needed to travel to work and to shops and schools. People often travelled by horse-drawn trams and buses. Early in the twentieth century, horse-drawn trams were replaced by electrical trams. The Luas in Dublin is a modern tram system, which opened in 2004. We also have buses of all shapes and sizes on our roads. Long-distance buses, called coaches, are often quite luxurious. They have curtains and reclining seats so that people can sleep. Some also have toilets, televisions and machines for making tea and coffee.

Horse-drawn tram, Dublin, 1896

Strand: Continuity and Change Over Time   Strand Unit: Transport

Hot History

In Japan, 'pushers' are employed in the stations. They push as many people as possible onto the trains!

Trains

When James Watt invented the steam engine in 1776, he probably had no idea that it would lead to trains that ran on steam. Steam engine trains allowed people, animals, coal and all kinds of goods to be transported over very long distances. Coal was used to heat the water that made the steam to power the engine. The early trains were huge, loud, smoky machines. In Ireland, there were 5500 km of railway tracks by 1920. The Dublin Area Rapid Transit (DART) began transporting people in 1984. The DART trains run along the coastline from Greystones, through Dublin City, to Howth. In some other big cities, trains run underground. For example, London has the Tube and Paris has the Métro. Some countries have trains that have no wheels at all! The maglev (short for 'magnetic levitation') trains in Germany are held onto the tracks by magnets.

Steam engine

Maglev train, Germany

Ships

Almost three-quarters of the earth's surface is covered by seas, oceans, lakes and rivers. For thousands of years, people tried to find the best way to travel across water. They began with rafts and hollowed-out tree trunks (dugout boats). Later, they made rowing boats. Strong muscles are needed for rowing, as the oars must be used to make the boat move. Around 3000 BC, sails were fitted onto boats so that they could be powered by the wind. For hundreds of years, sailing ships were used all over the world for transporting people and for trade. Some countries like England, France and Spain developed large fleets of ships, which they used for fighting battles. In the 1800s, steam ships began to be used. Steam was more reliable than the wind. Most modern ships have engines that are powered by diesel. Scientisits are now trying to develop ships that use wave power to make them move.

HMS Victory, British Royal Navy battleship, launched in 1759

Strand: Continuity and Change Over Time   Strand Unit: Transport

Traditional Irish boats

In Ireland, currachs have been used for transport and fishing for hundreds of years. Currachs are small, light boats made from wood and canvas, coated with tar. The tar helps to keep them waterproof. As far back as the 1700s, boats known as Galway hookers were used for fishing along the west coast of Ireland. They were also used to transport turf. Hookers have sails and they are bigger and heavier than currachs.

Galway hooker

Sea transport in Ireland

In the 1800s, many Irish people emigrated to Canada and the USA to escape the hunger and poverty in Ireland. The voyage was rough and it lasted for around 47 days. Some of the ships were not fit to go to sea. Because they were dirty and overcrowded, many people died of fever. Sometimes the ships sank in the middle of the ocean. They became known as 'coffin ships'. However, there were safe ships, too. The *Jeanie Johnston* was famous because no passenger ever died on board. James Attridge, the captain, cared for his passengers. He did not overcrowd the ship and he always had a doctor in his crew. In 1848, the *Jeanie Johnston* made its first trip from Blennerville, County Kerry, to Quebec, Canada, carrying 193 Irish emigrants. A replica of the *Jeanie Johnston* was built in 2002.

Replica of the Jeanie Johnston

The *Titanic*, which was built in Belfast, was powered by great steam engines and it was one of the most modern ships of its time. On its first voyage in April 1912, the *Titanic* struck an iceberg. It sank and 1517 lives were lost.

Rivers and canals

Rivers and canals (man-made rivers) have also been used to transport goods. The two best known canals in Ireland are the Royal and Grand Canals. They connect Dublin with the River Shannon and they were used to transport cargo (goods) to towns along the way. Horses were used to pull the early canal barges. They are now powered by engines.

Royal Canal

The first flights

How would you like to fly in a paper aeroplane? You might be surprised to learn that the first time a person travelled by air was in a hot-air balloon made from paper! The Montgolfier Brothers from France were the inventors of the balloon and in 1783, Étienne Montgolfier travelled above Paris for a distance of 9 km. The Wright Brothers made their first flight in 1903 in an aeroplane made from wooden frames covered in canvas. Orwell Wright travelled 37 m in 12 seconds, while his brother, Wilbur, looked on. In 1919, John Alcock and Arthur Brown made the first transatlantic flight, flying from Newfoundland, Canada, to Clifden, County Galway. The flight took 16 hours, 12 minutes.

The Wright Brothers' first flight

Hot History

When Charles Lindberg made the first solo flight from America to Europe in 1927, he had to cross the Atlantic Ocean. As his plane, the *Spirit of St Louis*, flew closer to Ireland, he saw some fishing boats off the coast of Kerry. He flew low, leaned out of the cockpit and asked the fishermen, "Which way to Ireland?"

Spirit of St Louis

Modern aircraft

Propellers are still used on small aeroplanes that are used for a variety of purposes, such as putting out forest fires, taking off and landing in places that have short runways and rescuing people in mountains. Large passenger planes like the Boeing 747, or the jumbo jet, as it is called due to its powerful jet engines, carry people all over the world. Helicopters are used to travel to places that are unsuitable for aeroplanes to land. Helicopters do not need a runway, so they can land in small spaces. They are often used for search and rescue missions, hovering while the victim is lifted to safety.

Boeing 747

Spacecraft

Endeavour, US space shuttle

The new frontier for modern transportation is outer space. In the past, sailors used the stars to navigate. Inventors developed telescopes to view the stars. Today, scientists make it possible to explore space by using satellites that send radio and television signals back to earth. Satellites are used to examine the surface of the Earth and even to spy on other countries! Astronauts have walked on the moon's surface and have brought matter back to Earth to be examined. In the future, planets like Mars and Jupiter will be investigated, too.

84 | Strand: Continuity and Change Over Time | Strand Unit: Transport

ACTIVITIES

A. Can You Remember?

1. When did the first railway start in Ireland? (Hint: Look at the timeline.)
2. What kind of fuel was used to power steam engines?
3. What was the first hot-air balloon made from?
4. James _____ invented the steam engine in _____.
5. When did Alcock and Brown make their transatlantic flight?

B. Choose the Correct Answer to Complete Each Sentence.

1. The wheel had been invented by _____.
   A. 200 AD, B. 2000 BC, C. 2000 AD, or D. 200 BC.
2. The best aircraft for search and rescue missions are _____.
   A. jumbo jets, B. Galway hookers, C. helicopters, or D. space shuttles
3. Horse-power is used to measure _____.
   A. distance, B. speed, C. weight, or D. energy
4. The first solo transatlantic flight was made by _____.
   A. John Alcock, B. Amy Johnson, C. Arthur Brown, or D. Charles Lindberg

C. Think About It.

1. Pair work: *People in the past were much better inventors than we are now.* Do you agree or disagree? Discuss it with your partner and then write your answer.
2. (a) Name the two materials that were used to make both currachs and early aeroplanes.
   (b) Why do you think those materials were used?
3. What forms of transport have we got in common with our ancestors?

D. Get Creative.

1. Find out where and how the following animals are used for travel and transport.
   (a) ox, (b) elephant, (c) llama, (d) yak, (e) husky
2. You are a member of the crew on the *Jeanie Johnston*. Write about your life and work on board and describe the passengers and the captain.

E. Digging Deeper

1. Check out the library or the internet to find out more about: John Alcock, Charles Lindbergh, Charles Bianconi, the *Jeanie Johnston*.
2. Group work: Make a list of 10 jobs that are associated with transport. Which one would you choose? Write the reasons for your choice and present them to the class.

Strand: Continuity and Change Over Time   Strand Unit: Transport

Unit 17: Tom Crean

New Words
exploration · expedition · navigation · pack ice

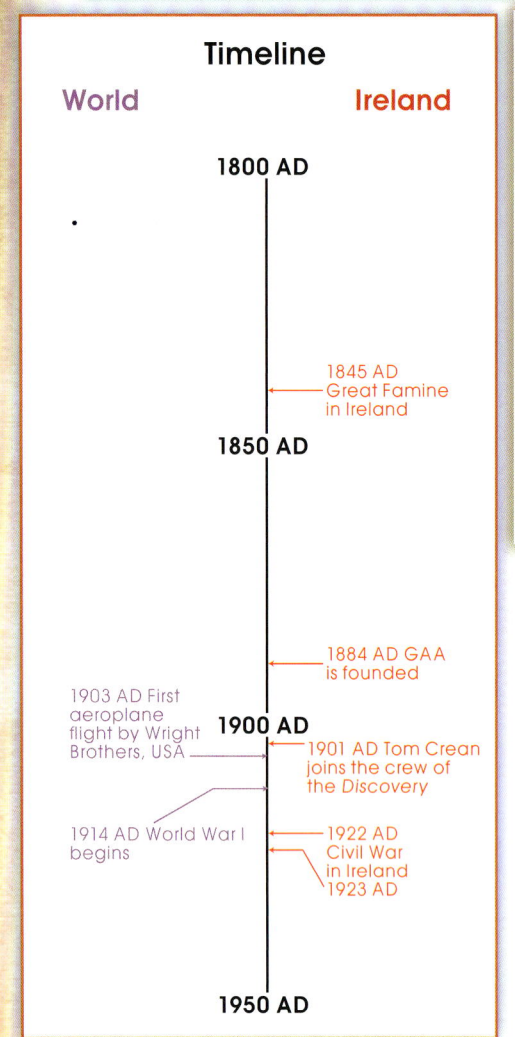

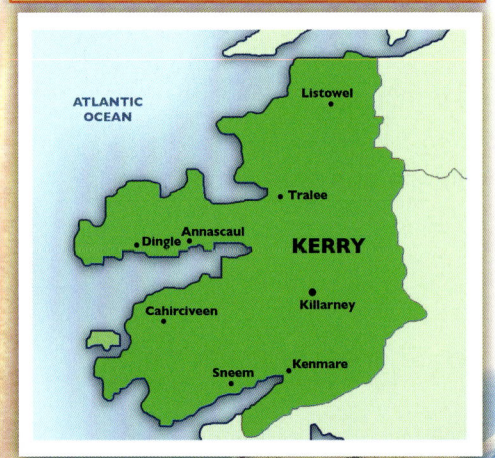

Timeline

World | **Ireland**

- 1800 AD
- 1845 AD Great Famine in Ireland
- 1850 AD
- 1884 AD GAA is founded
- 1903 AD First aeroplane flight by Wright Brothers, USA
- 1900 AD
- 1901 AD Tom Crean joins the crew of the *Discovery*
- 1914 AD World War I begins
- 1922 AD Civil War in Ireland 1923 AD
- 1950 AD

Tom Crean

Tom's Early Life

Tom Crean was born in 1877 AD close to the village of Annascaul in County Kerry. Tom's parents were farmers. Life on the land was difficult. At that time, children often left school at 12 years of age to find work. When Tom was 15 years old, he met an officer from the British Navy in the nearby town of Dingle. The officer was looking for young men to join the Navy. The British Navy was the most powerful navy in the world and it needed lots of young men to work on its ships. Young Tom thought that joining the Navy would be better than working on the land. He left home and travelled to Cobh, County Cork, to sign up as a Junior Seaman. In the early years, he worked on a number of ships and he even sailed as far as Japan. At Christmas, 1901, his ship was moored in New Zealand beside a British exploration ship called the *Discovery*. The *Discovery* was on its way to the Antarctic, more than 3000 km away.

Hot History
Tom Crean had to lie about his age in order to join the Navy. Recruits had to be at least 16 years old, but Tom was only 15! No one ever checked his age!

Antarctica

Strand: Story Strand Unit: Stories from the Lives of People in the Past

THE DISCOVERY

Tom got a job on board the *Discovery* and he became a member of Captain Robert Falcon Scott's crew. Tom joined an expedition to reach the South Pole. He soon got a taste of what life in the Antarctic was like. As they sailed south, the crew realised that this place was unlike anywhere else. The seas on the Southern Ocean were the roughest in the world and fierce storms were very common. After eight months at sea, the *Discovery* reached the coast of Antarctica in January, 1902. The ship got stuck in the ice, so the crew built a strong wooden hut for a base camp.

Discovery

Captain Scott

Hut Point, Antarctica

The *Discovery* crew's hut

DISCOVERY BASE CAMP

They settled down in the hut at the base camp and stayed there during the six months of winter darkness. During this long, dark time, it was very important to keep busy. Each man had his own special tasks to do. They included things like 'watering ship'. This involved cutting out blocks of ice and taking them on board the ship to be melted by the ship's boiler. This provided the men with a steady supply of drinking water. It was very difficult for them to get exercise, as the storms and blizzards forced them to stay in the hut for days on end. They celebrated their birthdays, which helped to pass the time. Some of the men played cards and chess and read books. When spring finally arrived, the crew got ready to head inland. In October of 1902, a group of men led by Captain Scott and Ernest Shackleton left the hut. Seaman Tom Crean was among the group.

Captain Scott's birthday dinner!

Hot Geography

The Ross Ice Shelf is about the size of France and it is the largest ice shelf in Antarctica. It fills a large bay at the entrance to the South Pole.

Heading south

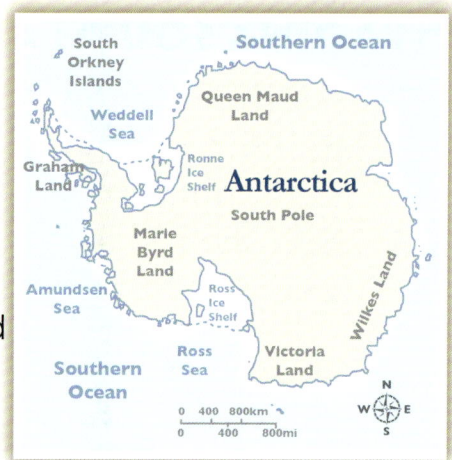

The group headed south towards the Ross Ice Shelf. However, they got less than halfway to the South Pole before some of the men were too tired to go on. They returned to base and found that their ship was stuck in the ice again. The Navy had to send a rescue ship. They used explosives to blast the ship clear of the ice. The *Discovery* arrived back in New Zealand in 1904. The crew had been away for two years.

The Terra Nova

A few years later, Captain Scott started to plan a new trip. He wanted to be the first to reach the South Pole and he lost no time in asking Tom Crean to join him on his new ship, the *Terra Nova* (meaning 'new land'), in 1910. When the *Terra Nova* arrived in Australia to get supplies, Captain Scott got a shock. Roald Amundsen, a famous Norwegian explorer, was planning to race them to the South Pole! The *Terra Nova* and Amundsen's ship, the *Fram*, both set sail from Australia at the same time. After six months of gale force winds and hurricanes, the *Terra Nova* finally reached the coast of Antarctica. The sailors immediately built a base camp in a spot that they named Cape Evans. The ship returned to Australia.

Terra Nova

Cape Evans base camp

The men prepared for the long dark months of winter by mending sleeping bags and making sledges. They hardly ever went outside and when they did, they were careful not to travel too far from the hut. All they could do was wait for the sun to appear and think about the race to the South Pole, which would be a journey of 2800 km.

Captain Scott in the Cape Evans base camp

Strand: Story   Strand Unit: Stories from the Lives of People in the Past

Heading south again

On November 1st, 1911, Scott and a group of men that included Tom Crean left the base camp at Cape Evans and headed south. Scott's plan was to use ponies and dogs to pull the sledges for the first part of the journey. After that, they planned to pull the sledges themselves. The last part of the journey was the Polar Plateau, where the men faced the coldest temperatures and the strongest winds. By December 20th, 1911, they were halfway across the Plateau. The air was getting thinner and they were gasping for breath. Two weeks later, with 240 km to go to reach the South Pole, Scott decided that only he and four others would try to complete the final part of the journey. Tom Crean was not in the group.

Tom Crean with sledge-dog puppies

Hot History
Tom Crean was known as the Irish Giant as he was quite a tall man!

Heroism

Tom Crean and his friends headed back towards the base camp, but one of the men named Edgar Evans became very ill and he had to be strapped onto his sledge. When they were about 56 km away from the base camp, William Lashey said that he would stay with Evans, while Tom went on alone to get help. Tom had no compass for navigation and no sleeping bag or tent for shelter. After walking non-stop for 19 hours, he reached base camp at 03:30 on the morning of February 19th, just as a storm began. He was exhausted and numb from the cold, but he immediately gave directions to the others. A rescue party was sent out and Evans and Lashey were saved.

Captain Scott and the other four men reached the South Pole a few weeks later, but Amundsen had got there one month earlier on January 19th, 1912. On the journey back to the base camp, Captain Scott and his men died. The *Terra Nova* picked up the survivors and returned to England. King George V awarded Tom Crean the Albert Medal for lifesaving. His march back to the base camp is said to be one of the greatest journeys of Polar explorers.

Cape Evans base camp

Strand: Story Strand Unit: Stories from the Lives of People in the Past

The Endurance

Ernest Shackleton

In 1914, Ernest Shackleton, who had been on the *Discovery* with Tom Crean, said that he was planning an expedition. He planned to walk from coast to coast across Antarctica. He asked Tom Crean to join his crew and in August 1914, they set off on the *Endurance*. On the way to Antarctica, the *Endurance* had to sail through lots of pack ice (floating ice). After 36 days, the crew spotted the Antarctic coast on January 10th, 1915. However, they were too far north to land. They kept going south, but on February 14th, the *Endurance* got stuck in the ice.

Rescue mission

The crew waited through the months of darkness, but after the sun returned in August, the ship remained stuck in the ice. After almost a year, the planks on the ship began to expand and buckle. The crew had to abandon ship and save their supplies. They waited on the sea ice until the ice began to break up beneath them. On April 8th, 1916, they took to the sea in lifeboats. They sailed for five days until they saw a huge rock, where they could land. They had reached Elephant Island. They survived there by eating seals and penguins and taking shelter under their upturned lifeboats. Shackleton decided to sail to South Georgia (more than 1200 km away) to get help. He set sail with Tom Crean and three others in a lifeboat called the *James Caird*. Three months later, they arrived back at Elephant Island to rescue the rest of the crew. All 27 of the men who had sailed on the *Endurance* made it home alive.

Hot History
Shackelton said that while they were sailing on the *James Caird*, Tom "always sang when he was steering, and nobody ever discovered what the song was ... but somehow it was cheerful."

The James Caird leaving Elephant Island

At home in Kerry

Tom Crean returned to Kerry in March 1920. He opened the South Pole Inn, where he lived with his wife and their three daughters. The pub is still open and people travel from all over the world to see the home of the great explorer and hero of the ice.

South Pole Inn, Annascaul

ACTIVITIES

A. Can You Remember?

1. At what age did Tom Crean join the British Navy?
2. How did the crew prepare for the winter after the *Terra Nova* reached Antarctica?
3. Name the Norwegian explorer who reached the South Pole before Captain Scott.
4. Why was Tom Crean awarded the Albert Medal?
5. Why did the crew of the *Endurance* abandon ship?

B. Choose the Correct Answer to Complete Each Sentence.

1. In Antarctica, winter lasts for _____.
   A. six days, B. six months, C. 12 months, or D. six years
2. Amundsen reached the _____ first.
   A. North Pole, B. Arctic, C. South Pole, or D. Antarctic
3. There were _____ on Elephant Island.
   A. penguins, B. polar bears, C. walruses, or D. elephants
4. Tom Crean was born in _____.
   A. 1787, B. 1977, C. 1877, or D. 1910

C. Think About It.

1. Why do you think explorers wanted to go to Antarctica?
2. Write two reasons why the explorers built base camps.
3. Do you think Tom Crean was unlucky? Give reasons for your answer.
4. Why did Tom Crean not stop for a rest on his 19-hour journey?

D. Get Creative.

1. Act out the scene between Tom Crean, Shackleton and the crew before they left Elephant Island.
2. Write a letter from a sailor on the *Terra Nova* to his family in Australia.
3. Make a class frieze showing the life of Tom Crean.
4. Imagine that you are one of the crew members left behind on Elephant Island. Write a page for your diary telling how you feel while waiting for help to arrive.

E. Digging Deeper

1. Check out the library or the internet to find out more about the Antarctic explorers.
2. For more information about the life of Tom Crean, read *Tom Crean: Ice Man* by Michael Smith.
3. Use the internet to follow the trail of Tom Crean. Your teacher will give you a list of words to key into a search engine.

Strand: Story   Strand Unit: Stories from the Lives of People in the Past

Unit 18: My Family

New Words

generation   evidence   documents   birth certificate   registered   artefacts   tradition   family tree

Timeline

World | **Ireland**

1850 AD
- 1851 AD Card game of Happy Families is invented
- 1852 AD Fossett Family begin Ireland's first circus
- 1870 AD Mothering Sunday begins in the USA

1900 AD
- 1908 AD Father's Day begins in the USA
- 1935 AD The Austrian Trapp Family Choir sings in public
- 1937 AD Irish law says that parents are the first teachers of their children

1950 AD
- 1954 AD Universal Children's Day is first celebrated in Switzerland
- 1965 AD Charlie Chaplin and his family come to live in Ireland
- 1978 AD National Grandparents' Day begins in the USA
- 1992 AD The Irish State promises to protect the rights of children

2000 AD

Imagine how happy everyone was on the day you were born. Your parents were delighted with you. If you had brothers and sisters, they were very excited to see the tiny, new baby. Since then, many things have happened in your life. You have grown. You can now do lots of things you could not do when you were younger. It is more than four years since you started in Junior Infants and you are now in the senior part of your school. Time marches on! You can see that even during one school day. There are different activities in the morning, at midday and in the afternoon. When home time comes, the calling of the roll in the morning seems a long way away. Your school timetable is like a timeline of daily activities: morning ➡ afternoon ➡ evening ➡ night: the history of the day! You can also think of your own life like a timeline: from being a baby, to a toddler, to the person you are now. Lots of different and interesting things have happened along the way.

Generations

Your parents were once babies. They are from the age group, or generation, that went before us. Your grandparents are from the generation before that and so on, back through time and history! In the past, family members from different generations tended to live near each other. Some still do. Others live in different places around the world. Wherever they live, each generation can help the others in different ways.

Three generations of a family

92   **Strand:** Local Studies   **Strand Unit:** My Family

We can make a timeline for the generations in our families. For example:

Grandparents are born ➡ school ➡ job ➡ marry ➡ children (my parents) ➡ school ➡ job ➡ marry ➡ children (me!) ➡ school ➡ the future…

Oral evidence

A detective looks for clues, or evidence, to find the answer to a mystery. You must also look for evidence to find out about the events in your history. Special occasions, such as your first day at school and last year's birthday party are quite easy to remember. Can you remember getting your first tooth and taking your first steps? Probably not! Those are the events that your parents or other important adults in your life can tell you about. They remember lots of details and stories about you from when you were very young. We call this oral evidence.

Hot History

In medieval times, families became known by their trade. Blacksmiths became known as 'Smith'. Carpenters were called 'Carpenter'. Barrel makers were known as 'Cooper'.

Pictorial evidence

Another place we can get information is from photographs. We call this pictorial evidence. Photographs can answer some of our questions, but not all of them. Look at the photograph to the left. What evidence in the picture might make us decide that the baby is a girl? Why do you think the photograph was taken? Who do you think took it? Can you be sure of your answers?

Documents

A third and very important source of information is documents, such as newspaper notices, baby books and birth certificates. After a baby is born, the law says that its birth must be recorded, or registered, in a special office. A birth certificate is a very important document, as it has details such as the baby's name, the date of its birth and its parents' names. It is a very reliable source of information.

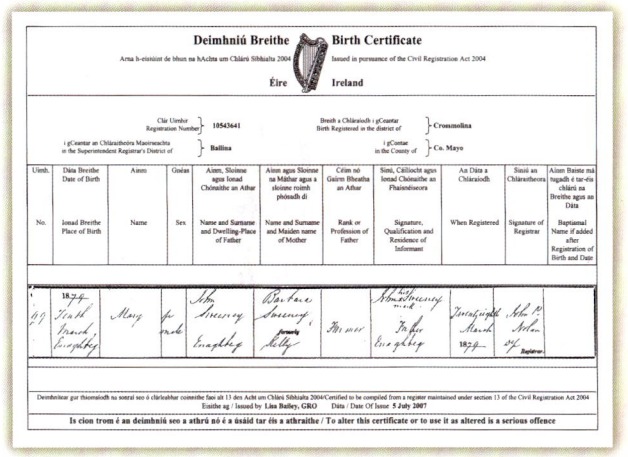

Birth certificate of Mary Sweeney, 1879, Enaghbeg, Crossmolina, County Mayo

Hospital nametag

Hospital nametags also provide information such as the time and place of birth, gender, birth-weight and name of the baby.

Strand: Local Studies   Strand Unit: My Family

FAMILY ARTEFACTS

A family photo album is a great place to see what everyone looked like years ago. Look at Uncle Joe wearing a bonnet! Artefacts (things from the past) such as toys, baby clothes and equipment are another good source of information. Look at the photographs of the prams below and their dates. See how they can give us historical information. Everyday objects can give us a lot of information about changes that have taken place over time.

Uncle Joe age 10 months

Aunt Molly's First Communion

1900   1950   2013

FAMILY TRADITIONS

A tradition is something that is passed on from generation to generation. For example, it is a tradition in Ireland to have a Saint Patrick's Day parade. The way in which a family celebrates important occasions like births and marriages depends a lot on their country's traditions.

FAMILY TREE

You can record all of the people who belong to your family by using a diagram known as a family tree. Look at Tom Murphy's family tree. Note: We use the word 'paternal' when we are talking about fathers. This is because the Latin (Ancient Roman language) word for father is *pater*. Can you guess what the Latin word for mother is?

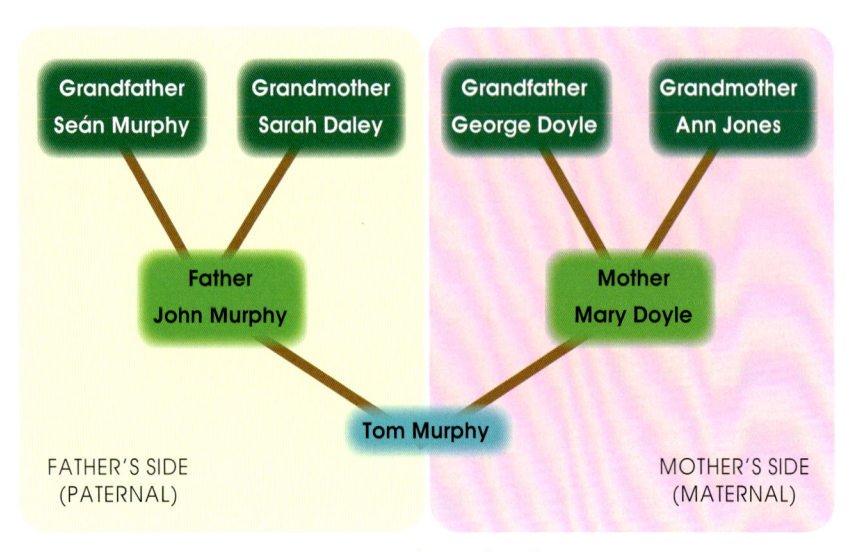

Grandfather Seán Murphy — **Grandmother** Sarah Daley
Grandfather George Doyle — **Grandmother** Ann Jones
Father John Murphy
Mother Mary Doyle
Tom Murphy

FATHER'S SIDE (PATERNAL)   MOTHER'S SIDE (MATERNAL)

Tom Murphy's family tree

ACTIVITIES

A. Can You Remember?

1. In what year did Mothering Sunday begin? (Hint: Look at the timeline.)
2. What was the name of the family that started Ireland's first circus?
3. How long is it since the first Father's Day was celebrated?
4. What information would you find on a baby's hospital nametag?
5. Where was Universal Children's Day first celebrated?

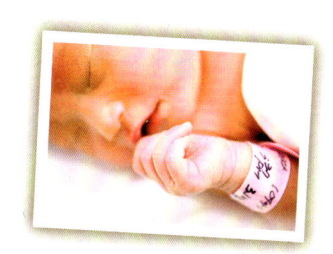

B. Choose the Correct Answer to Complete Each Sentence.

1. Pictorial evidence comes from _____.
   A. DVDs, B. photographs, C. toys, or D. films
2. *Pater* is the Latin word for _____.
   A. source, B. father, C. Romans, or D. mother
3. The Irish State promised to protect the rights of children in _____.
   A. 1992, B. 1929, C. 2009, or D. 1299
4. A birth certificate is a _____.
   A. book, B. magazine, C. document, or D. notebook

C. Think About It.

1. Group work: Discuss the ways in which older and younger generations can help each other. Present your ideas to the class.
2. Pair work: Discuss the four types of evidence that we use in history (oral, pictorial, documents and artefacts). Which one do you think gives us the best information? Write the reason for your answer.

D. Get Creative.

1. Make your own timeline. Stick two sheets of A4 paper together lengthwise. Stick on a few photographs that were taken of you at different stages since you were a baby. Beneath each photograph, write the date and a few sentences to explain the event.
2. Many of the first stories we hear are about families, for example 'Cinderella', 'Red Riding Hood' and 'Hansel and Gretel'. Why do you think this is?
3. Write one story involving all of the characters from the fairytales mentioned above!

E. Digging Deeper

1. Read a novel from the *Little House* series by Laura Ingalls Wilder. The series is all about her family's life in Kansas, America.
2. Use the internet to investigate your ancestors. Your teacher will give you a list of words to key into a search engine.

Glossary

Abacus (Unit 11): A frame with tiny balls used for counting

Archaeologist (Unit 3): A person who studies ancient people through objects they have left behind

Artefact (Unit 7): An object from the past

Barter (Unit 7): Trading with goods instead of money

Battlements (Unit 13): An area on top of a castle, used to keep a lookout over the countryside

Blacksmith (Unit 5): A person who makes objects from iron

BC (Unit 2): Before Christ

Coffin ship (Unit 16): An unsafe transatlantic sailing ship

Cuneiform (Unit 4): A type of writing that uses patterns

Currach (Unit 7): A small boat made from wood and canvas and coated with tar to make it waterproof

Documents (Unit 18): Pieces of paper that give proof of something

Domesticated (Unit 3): No longer wild – tamed to live near people

Drawbridge (Unit 13): A bridge over a moat that could be lowered or raised

Dungeon (Unit 13): Cells under a castle, where prisoners were kept

Evidence (Unit 18): A reason to believe in something

Family tree (Unit 18): A diagram that shows how generations in a family relate to each other

Flint (Unit 2): A very hard stone

Fostering (11): Children living with families other than their own

Fulacht fiadh (Unit 7): A wood or stone pit, filled with water and used for cooking

Generation (Unit 18): All people born within the same time (about 30 years)

Gladiator (Unit 6): A person who fought (possibly to the death) in Roman times

Guild (Unit 14): A group of craftsmen with the same trade, for example, a carpenters' guild

Hedge schools (Unit 11): Open-air schools

Ice age (Unit 2): A time when Earth was covered in ice

Ludi (Unit 11): The word for schools in Ancient Rome

Mail (Unit 13): Body protection made of metal rings linked together

Manuscript (Unit 8): A handwritten book

Midden (Unit 2): A rubbish heap

Minstrels (Unit 13): Musicians

Motte and bailey (Unit 13): A defensive structure made of earth and timber or stone

Mummers (Unit 6): Actors

Nomad (Unit 2): A person who moves around to follow the supply of food

Plague (Unit 14): A terrible disease

Quern-stone (Unit 3): A pair of stones used to grind things like grain

Scroll (Unit 11): A roll of papyrus used as a page

Slate (Unit 11): A flat piece of grey stone used for writing on with chalk

Smelting (Unit 7): Using heat to melt metal from rock

Smith (Unit 4): A person who makes metal objects

Standing stones (Unit 7): Large upright stones, sometimes marking a Bronze Age grave

Stone circles (Unit 7): Stones set in a circle to mark burial places and/or the position of the sun and moon

Stylus (Unit 11): A tool used for writing in Ancient Rome

Trackway (Unit 7): Pathway

Tradition (Unit 18): A custom or belief handed down from one generation to the next

Wattle and daub (Unit 7): Sticks and mud used for making walls

Yoke (Unit 3): A wooden frame for joining farm animals together at their necks